THE MULTIPLYING
CHURCH

Other books by Bob Roberts Jr.

Transformation: How Glocal Churches Transform Lives and the World

Glocalization: How Followers of Jesus Engage a Flat World

glocalnet
Connecting for glocal transformation.

Visit www.glocal.net for more information and training
manuals for interns and church planters.

www.glocal.net

THE MULTIPLYING
CHURCH

THE NEW MATH
FOR STARTING
NEW CHURCHES

BOB ROBERTS JR.

ZONDERVAN.com/
AUTHORTRACKER
follow your favorite authors

We want to hear from you. Please send your comments about this book to us in care of zreview@zondervan.com. Thank you.

ZONDERVAN®

The Multiplying Church
Copyright © 2008 by Bob Roberts Jr.

Requests for information should be addressed to:

Zondervan, *Grand Rapids, Michigan 49530*

Library of Congress Cataloging-in-Publication Data

Roberts, Bob, 1958 –
    The multiplying church : the new math for starting new churches / Bob Roberts.
       p. cm.
    Includes bibliographical references and index.
    ISBN-13: 978-0-310-27716-3 (hardcover)
    ISBN-10: 0-310-27716-7 (hardcover)
    1. Church development, New. I. Title.
BV652.24.R58 2007
254'.1 – dc22

                        2007049181

Published in association with the literary and marketing agency of C. Grant and Company.

Interior design by Matthew Van Zomeren

Printed in the United States of America

---

08 09 10 11 12 13 • 10 9 8 7 6 5 4 3 2 1

Dedicated to

Bob Buford and Al Weiss
Twenty-first-century men from Cyrene and Cyprus who
are fueling church planting in the United States like no one else.

Church planters worldwide
You have taught me more about the faith and
church than I have ever taught you.

Every church planter from NorthWood
I love you guys deeply and am so proud of you.

CONTENTS

FIGURES

ACKNOWLEDGMENTS

Church multiplication has first and foremost been a family adventure of which Nikki, Ben, Jill, and Ti have all been a part of. Thank you, family, for sharing me with other cities around the world. Thank you for long lunches with planters and strategists where you sat patiently after several services on Sundays. Nikki, you have matched me — step for step. Your ministry to church planters and pastors' wives has not been without fruit — way to go. You are a great preacher and leader!

NorthWood — you like makin' babies! I pray for a day in the not-too-distant future when we are starting twenty-five churches a year out of this place all over the world.

The entire staff of NorthWood — you have trained, taught, mentored, coached, and encouraged tens of thousands from investing in dozens of young planters.

Johnnie Morgan — this is your ministry as much as anyone's. Without you, there is no way NorthWood or I could do all that we have.

Bob Buford, Linda Stanley, and Dave Travis — thanks for believing in me and giving me a shot at growing the ministry.

I never knew it took so many people to get a book written and published. Thanks to Chris Grant, Mary Ann Lackland, Mike Cook, Paul Engle, and Verlyn Verbrugge.

This year's interns — this was a turning point, and you helped us make it: Bald Bobby Vaughn, Global Paul Watson, Handsome Richie Kim, Rooster Donnie Featherston, Bhudda Matt Allen, Liberian Chandler Freeman, Pueblan Gabriel Alfaro, Horse-Racin' Tim Doremus, Milk Chocolate Enthusiast David Rush, Smart Dr. Bob Garret, American-Only-Food-Eater Bill Wilson, and Ricky Bobby Gonna Reach Travis Dunham.

Special thanks also go to the Vision360 Board members listed below: Al Weiss, Steve Johnson, Jerry Sheveland, Paul Johnson, John Jenkins, Terry Roussel, Tom and DeAnne Hutchison, Ken Lockard, Dan Johnson, Leonard Buhler, and Erwin McManus.

FOREWORD

Kingdom-minded leaders stop focusing on what is hard or risky, move beyond the comfort of addition within their own building — and risk.

My friend Bob Roberts is a risk taker. It is evident in his ministry. As a result of shunning the safe in favor of radically chasing after the Kingdom of God, Bob has become a multiplier. He has instilled that mentality in the members of NorthWood Church, the body of believers he pastors in Keller, Texas. The result: exponential Kingdom growth.

Not many people are able to grasp what it means to think and act exponentially, especially in today's North American church. But, Bob is there on both. That is what makes him uniquely qualified to share his insights. I can be pretty frantic, but I pause when I hear or read something that comes from somebody who's "been there, done that." Bob has always given me reason to pause.

Actually, I did more than pause when Bob sent me this latest book, *The Multiplying Church*. I lingered. Bob explains what the church should look like when it fulfills the biblical mission of reaching the people of the world for Christ. When the church lives out its mission, it will be founded on the gospel, evidence true discipleship, positively impact society, and become the body of Christ in whatever cultural context it develops. Ministry will be done. Jesus will be worshiped as supreme above all else. People will be prepped for the Feast of the Land.

And it will be done in accelerating fashion.

Really, Bob describes what can happen when "Missional Meets Exponential." Jesus loves the church and gave himself for her (Eph. 5:25). He declares, "I will build my church" (Matt. 16:18). Moreover, he allows us to join him in its building. Following our Lord's command to make disciples of all the "nations" (Matt. 28:19–20) and to witness for him throughout the world (Acts 1:8), the Bible records the acts of the apostles as planting churches, evangelizing, and teaching the new believers.

In Acts 20:28, Paul exhorted the elders of the church at Ephesus "to shepherd the church of God" (HCSB), meaning that they should care for and guard the church. In fact, he emphasizes that point earlier in that verse ("Be on guard for yourselves and for all the flock"). In 1 Corinthians 14, Paul encouraged the leaders in Corinth to edify, build up, and strengthen the church through worship.

I have seen it time and time again in research I've conducted. Churches that multiply exponentially have pastors who constantly encourage members to get out where real people with real problems live and *be* Christ; they stress: *Be the church Jesus intended*. Of course in admonishing this, these pastors have not unlocked the secrets to quantum physics. They're simply repeating a recurring theme of Jesus' ministry. He doesn't call us to stagnation. The Savior was constantly pressing forward into the spiritual darkness and charging his charges to charge! They were to go!

Interestingly Jesus was intentional. There was no winning converts for the sake of boosting numbers at the First Church of Jerusalem. If that had been his interest, he would have made a church like too many twenty-first-century evangelical churches and glossed it all over with those groupies he alienated. No, Jesus had building the Kingdom of God locked squarely in his sights. Paul understood the primacy of Jesus' objective better than any other human who has lived. He gave his life for the birth, growth, and multiplication of the church.

Bob has that same kind of passion for seeing churches live out that same mission. He codes it into the DNA of a church plant. At the heart of Bob's vision for church planting is developing leadership that will plant churches with the intention of planting other churches. NorthWood Church offers a nine-month internship where Bob annually trains more than a dozen potential church planters and their spouses. Since Scripture nowhere says that "Caucasians will inherit the Kingdom," Bob is intentional about making sure half the internships are filled with non-Anglo planters who reach other ethnic groups both within the United States and beyond. These church planters are not locked into programmed models but instead focus first on the needs of the community and allow cultural flavor to influence the form of church. The beauty is that the gospel is at the heart, bringing a standardization to otherwise radically diverse sister churches.

You will find a discussion of these things in this book. Bob teaches how missional churches act faithfully and intentionally wherever God gives them opportunity by being incarnational, indigenous, and intentional. Let me spell this out so it's even clearer where Bob is heading:

Incarnational: Missional churches become deeply involved in their communities. They are not focused so much on their buildings as they are on living, demonstrating, and offering biblical community in a lost world among a lost people. An incarnational church functions as the "body of Christ" because it represents the presence of Christ within a community. They get that the reason spiritually lost people act spiritually lost is because, well, they *are* spiritually lost. They don't back away from godless people but instead embrace godless people because they understand the hearts of lost people conquered by the lordship of Jesus builds the Kingdom.

Indigenous: Missional churches take root in the soil of their society and reflect, appropriately, their surrounding culture. Obvious example: If a church is in an urban setting saturated with hip-hop culture, southern gospel quartets miss the mark. Bob teaches this. Related (WARNING: toe-stomping zone ahead): It's ironic that most evangelical churches are filled with people who live very much like the world but look different from it on Sunday. Study after study has shown that many North American evangelicals engage in the same lifestyles and sins as the unchurched. It should be exactly the opposite—we should look similar to those in our community but act like members of a heavenly community.

Intentional: Missional churches are intentional about their methodologies. In missional churches, biblical preaching, discipleship, baptism, and other functions are vital. But worship style, evangelistic methods, attire, service times, locations, and other matters are determined by their effectiveness in a specific cultural context. (I know this last statement probably turns some dogmatic theological cranks out there, but before you get too worked up leave your cultural presuppositions outside your prayer closet and spend a little time objectively reviewing Romans 14 and the first half of 15. Paul had lots to say about primary and secondary issues, and we would do well to keep our Bibles open there before being too critical of churches actually multiplying themselves among people different than themselves.)

There are two key factors that mark Bob and this book.

(1) When Jesus proclaimed, "As the Father has sent me, so send I you" (John 20:21), his mandate was not directed to a select group of cross-cultural missionaries. It was a commissioning act of you, me, and our churches as well. We have a sender (Jesus), a message (the gospel) and a people to whom we are sent (those in our culture). I call this *becoming missional in practice* or *missional orthopraxy.* "Being sent" means that we must move outside the walls of our church buildings and engage the people in our communities.

Bob models spiritual transformation personally and leads others to experience transformation that results in spiritual obedience. They are changed ... and when they are changed they change their world. They are missional in practice.

(2) Growth is a spiritual work granted by God (Heb. 6:3), not a mechanistic formula. John Mark Terry explains, "We have the best materials, media, and methods, but we lack spiritual power. Christians of the apostolic era had none of our advantages; they didn't even have the New Testament. Still, they turned the Roman Empire upside down. What impact does your church have in your community?"[1]

In the book of Revelation, Jesus evaluates seven churches and reveals a pattern for evaluating churches throughout history. If you look around your city today, you will most likely find churches that face challenges like the church at Ephesus, resemble the church at Laodicea, and endure false teaching like the church at Thyatira. Jesus, as Head of his church, evaluates us and calls us to repentance when we lose our proper focus (Heb. 12:2). He was *evaluating based on spiritual impact.* Bob's book causes me to evaluate my life, my ministry, my church planting — everything — based on the spiritual impact I'm having on the world around me. George Barna also reflects on this issue of spiritual impact and leadership:

> After fifteen years of diligent digging into the world around me, I have reached several conclusions about the future of the Christian church in America. The central conclusion is that the American church is dying due to lack of strong spiritual leadership. In this time of unprecedented opportunity and plentiful resources, the church is actually losing influence. The primary reason is the lack of leadership. Nothing is more important than leadership.[2]

I made the statement at the beginning of this foreword that Kingdom-minded leaders stop focusing on what is hard or risky, move beyond the comfort of addition within their own building, and risk. This takes courage, and I think what Barna is ultimately getting at is that there are not enough people with courage to give themselves to the cause of reversing the trend and leading the church into the fray of contemporary culture unapologetically wielding the Sword of Truth (which is the Bible).

Jesus wants risk takers. He calls for courage. He expects us to be like him. "I tell you the truth, anyone who has faith in me will do what I have been doing. He will do even greater things than these, because I am going to the Father. And I will do whatever you ask in my name, so that the Son may bring glory to the Father. You may ask me for anything in my name, and I will do it" (John 14:12 – 14). Jesus had the opportunity to only physically impact his own culture and geographic region. But he has given to us the opportunity to have a global impact. The question is, "Do we have the courage to build his Kingdom?" If talking about building the Kingdom was sufficient, I can tell you the curtain would have dropped and the show ended a long time ago. Courage and action are synonyms.

If we are going to move from missional to exponential, it will be costly. It will cost something financially — giving beyond what we think is reasonable. It will cost something spiritually — praying longer than we feel like praying. It will cost something mentally and emotionally — sending out workers into his harvest fields is hard to do because we have to let go of things and people that are dear to us (or at least dear to our earthly kingdoms). It will cost us something physically — being disciplined in every area of life is difficult.

Bob knows that transformation of society can happen — he's seen it happen in more than a hundred church plants — but he knows it only happens when the gospel impacts the culture. In the end, Bob helps bring us back in a simple but profound way to the fundamental truth in Scripture—it all boils down to Jesus. He guarantees the forces of hell won't stand against his church (Matt. 16:18); he gave his peace to his disciples (hint: *us*) and then said, "Go" (John 20:21). He is the builder, the sender, the head, the beginning, and the end of it all. There is no other name under heaven given among men by which people can be saved (Acts 4:12), and it is at the pronouncement of this precious name, and this precious name alone—"Jesus!"—that every knee will someday bow and every tongue will confess that he is Lord, to the glory of God the Father.

May his name be lifted high from our lips and in our churches. May his fame spread to the ends of the earth.

Ed Stetzer, director of LifeWay Research
and missiologist in residence

Notes

1. John Mark Terry. *Church Evangelism* (Nashville: Broadman & Holman, 1997), 16.

2. George Barna, *Leaders on Leadership* (Ventura, CA: Regal, 1997), 18.

FOREWORD

In his first book, *Transformation*, Bob set out a vision for a discipleship that has the world, as well as the local church, in mind. He contended that the transformed human must lead to a transformed humanity. His primary focus in that book remained on the individual, but he nonetheless constantly pointed us outward to the world beyond the local church, city, and nation, to what he calls *the glocal world*—the highly interconnected reality in which all of us live. Bob envisions a new way of engaging the glocal to achieve common goals. He calls it "domain jumping"—the willingness to join the kingdom agenda within the different domains of life (e.g., education, politics, religion, economics, art) and not limit mission and ministry to the religious, or churchly, sphere. In his mind, mission involves a seriously expansive agenda.

In *Glocalization* Bob developed his ideas further but focused the reader on the radically changing social, political, economic, and cultural patterns of the world in which we are called to live and love. Drawing inspiration from early church history and the emerging church in the developing world, he calls us to reconstruct a new missional operating system rather than a church program. He proposes ten major glocal issues that demand our attention: communicable disease, hunger, water and sanitation, corruption, migration and refugees, climate change, education, armed conflict, economy, and trade subsidies. Clearly in this book the agenda moves beyond the narrow concerns of "the church."

In this present book Bob Roberts not only lays out a vision of a multiplying (and multipli-*able*) church that can operate in the glocal context, but also suggests practical ways we can actually begin the journey to multiplication church planting. Make no mistake; most churches in the West are beginners in this regard and need his guidance. We know from history and experience that a genuine encounter with Jesus results in movements that change the world. If this is so, then multiplication church planting must become a vital part of the missional equation. The twenty-first century requires that we adopt a movement ethos and approach, and *The Multiplying Church* is Bob Roberts' valuable contribution to the missional agenda of God's people in God's world.

But what intrigues me the most, and what is perhaps of most importance in the work of Bob Roberts, is that the man himself is well worthy of study and emulation. Bob has an innate capacity to accumulate important ideas and reconfigure them in ways that the average person can grasp. Indeed, he is a well-read, intelligent man. I have had wonderfully wide-ranging discussions with him on numerous occasions, and he is disarmingly bright. But what is distinctive about him is that as a genuine practitioner he does not stop at the ideas-in-themselves. His more primal instincts (thank God) are *application* as well as *demonstration*, and it is here where he makes his greatest contribution.

Bob Roberts is a genuine apostolic pioneer—the *real deal*. Honestly, it is exceedingly hard to find anyone comparable with Bob in the world today. Where does one find a big Texan pastor engaging effectively where diplomats fear to tread? Which Southern Baptist preacher do we know who gets to meet prime ministers, presidents, warlords, political dissidents, mullahs, or whatever, and somehow brings them together and gets them talking peace? Which local pastor *anywhere* is involved in "nation-building" (his phrase) in ways that he is? And where do we find a conservative evangelical like Bob addressing glocal issues with such practical compassion while keeping the living message of Jesus, as well as active missionary church planting, at the center of the equation?

I ask again, who goes where Bob goes and does what he does? And with the silence that flows from that question I rest my case: the man is worth listening to because God is doing something unique in and through him. We *must* pay attention.

Alan Hirsch, author of The Forgotten Ways *and*
The Shaping of Things to Come, *and founding*
director of Forge Mission Training Network

PREFACE

Writing a book on church multiplication is like describing Texas weather today in anticipation of what it will be tomorrow. It is always changing. There is no such thing as a comprehensive book on church planting. If there were, it would be huge, and it would also be dated quickly. If people are going to plant a church, they must be entrepreneurial not only in their plant, but also in their learning. The same is true of pastors who want to plant multiple churches out of their local churches. It is a never-ending study.[1]

This book is no exception. *But it isn't about just starting a church.* Instead, I focus on understanding how movements take place and how we might see one begin in the United States. I'm also taking it a step further to talk about how local churches begin mothering other churches, resulting in church multiplication.

One of the great tragedies today is that so few churches in America are multiplying. Ed Stetzer recently did a research project in which he identified the top church planting churches in America. He says, "I am somewhat surprised that getting to be one of the top 100 church planting churches is not that hard—there are just not that many true multiplying churches in North America."[2] It was disappointing and disheartening to him because in the current state, a church doesn't have to do a whole lot to be a part of the top tier.

For too long the focus has been exclusively on the planter and the new church. I think we have forgotten two important links without which we will never get to movement status. Those links are the role of the disciple and the role of the mother church.

In the past we have been operating this way:

Planter → New Church

This is fine if all we want is addition. However, if you want to see multiplication—with a passion to see a movement happen—we are going to have to begin to think differently. Something like this:

Disciple → Mother Church → Planter → New Church

What is exciting about this is that everybody gets to play. I've been at conferences where an exciting young church planter begins to talk about what he or she is doing that inspires more young entrepreneurial planters to do the same thing. However, I've seen sadness creep over the faces of less entrepreneurial or older pastors who know that will never be their story. That doesn't need to be the case. A planter is one. A mother has many. Every church can get into the church planting arena when we think of it in a new light. Better to be a mother who produces ten than a planter who produces one. The real key to a church planting movement doesn't lie in the individual church that is planted, but in the incubators that produce churches.

In truth, you're a church planter only a couple of years; after that, you're a pastor. My heart has broken on numerous occasions when I've been with a planter who really believes in church planting—as long as they're planting. Once they're established, sadly, they don't start any more new churches.

Church planting is what *I* do. Church multiplication is what *we* do. Church planting is *my* story. Church multiplication is *our* story. In America, we focus on planters and church planting organizations, when we ought to focus primarily on churches multiplying churches on a regular basis. The future of faith in America (and anywhere in the world, for that matter) is not tied to planting more churches, but in the raising up of mother congregations of every tribe, tongue, denomination, and network that are reproducing like rabbits. Until that happens, we are only a dream waiting to happen. The individualistic, narcissistic, consumer mind-set that has gripped the church today is killing us. Nothing will cause adults to sacrifice all they have, even their lives, like their children. We need pastors and churches who care more about their children than they do about themselves. The only way to do that is to make babies.

I visited with a young minister yesterday who may not be a church planter but said, "I want to be at a church where we can plant lots of churches." He's expecting to be a part of a church-starting culture. The hope of the future of the church in the United States really is not in raising up more preachers; we've been doing that in high style for the past hundred years. The hope is in pregnant mother churches.

I remember when I first started NorthWood, driving people out to show them the piece of land where our church was to be. Then when we built our first building I'd show that with pride. I had no clue the incredible joy I'd have years later to drive in a community to visit the church of a young church planter who came out of our church.

My wife did one of those videos for my fortieth birthday that showed me as a baby, then as a child, then as a teen, and finally as a young adult and us and our family pictures. It was really great. However, what moved me to weeping were the pictures and greetings from the young church planters who had come out of our church.

It was as if God were speaking to me through that video, saying, "I've reserved you to raise up others." At last count, there are close to thirty thousand people in our church plants. They just don't fit in our building. We now have not just daughter churches, but granddaughter and great-granddaughter churches. Move over, Joel Osteen—Bobby Gene is on the way! I tell NorthWood frequently, as I did this past Sunday as we commissioned a young couple to plant, "It isn't about us and our church but about Jesus and his church—and his church is far bigger than this one single church."

The new math for understanding the concepts involved in starting new churches is based on some simple, creative formulas that I've given you in each chapter of this book. My family and friends who know me well are laughing at my using a mathematical metaphor. I hate math. I shouted with great joy for a C minus in algebra in college! The only thing I was ever good at in math, however, was multiplication. I remember sitting at a desk in the parsonage of the Westside Baptist Church in Corsicana, Texas, with my dad trying to teach me my multiplication tables. It took a long time, but something finally clicked and I got it.

It has taken far too long for the church to "get it" when it comes to understanding multiplication as the key to church planting in America and the West. It's not just a nice concept; it means the spiritual survival and viability of the church in the West.

Maybe I'm speaking to a brother or sister who is reading these words and we can pray together:

> *Father, break us of the way we have tied our egos to our ministries. Forgive us of wanting to be the superstars and the heroes. Forgive us for engaging in turfism and allowing our individual ministries to define your kingdom.*
>
> *May we see that your kingdom is beyond any one single local church, and may those of us that are pastors lead our churches in like manner.*
>
> *May our focus be for the love of you.*
>
> *May our mandate be to equip others to follow you.*
>
> *May the fruit of our hands be seen in a viral faith that is spreading all across our land through churches that are being multiplied.*
>
> *May the churches we plant play such a vital role in the healing of our cities and communities that nonbelieving leaders will beg us to come start churches where they are.*
>
> *When we stand and preach, or sit and share, may we see the young men and women whom you are calling out to multiply.*
>
> *May we challenge them, equip them, send them, and be there for them.*
>
> *May the story of our lives be not just what we have done, but what others have done as a result of how we have served them.*
>
> *May we serve with such humility that our names are barely known here.*
>
> *But may I stand before you one day when a great smile appears across your face and I hear you say, "Roberts — you're crazy, but good job. You did it, son — let's party!"*

Notes

1. I've provided a list of suggested reading in the back of this book in order to help begin that learning process.

2. Ed Stetzer, "Church Squared," *Outreach* magazine (July 2007).

PART 1

THE NEW MATH

Chapter 1

MADE IN ASIA — JESUS MOVEMENTS

CPM − CP + J = JM

Autumn in Hanoi, Vietnam

BEING MISSIONAL

Blog posted by Bob Roberts Jr.

I just returned from Vietnam where the church is exploding. What I have seen on this trip and in the past is a church growing not because of Western involvement (or any other that I could detect), but from unique stories of how individuals came to faith in Christ through unexpected ways and then wound up leading friends to faith in Christ. That led to them starting groups to pray and worship and reach out. I've yet to meet someone who deliberately set out to start a church. It just happened because they were leading their friends to faith in Christ — just like what happened in Acts 11. Church wasn't something they intentionally started to reach all these lost seekers. It was a community that developed and emerged from following Christ together.

Often at church planter gatherings I'll hear people say they wanted to start a church because they wanted to reach seekers — that's good. I'll hear them say they wanted to be a part of something fresh and new and more culturally relevant — that's good, too. Those that are theologically adept (like me!) will say they want to start churches to glorify God. The big thing now is to "start something missional" — obviously to me that's very good. But I've NEVER heard that in Vietnam or other countries where the Gospel is exploding sometimes under difficult situations.

It's the rage right now in the West though. We have built a whole religious industry around being missional, primarily for young pastors. But all of us feel the tug. Recently my speaking schedule began to get too full and cramp my schedule for how I'm actually on the ground at my home base and around the world working. In other words, I had to choose to "speak" missional or "do" missional!

At best, in the West we've tried to implement a few things or activities that we hope are "missional." Yet those who are experiencing it don't realize it; they can't explain it — but they are it! Neither could they give a lecture on it.

You can't find talks, lectures, research, explanations, or steps on what is "missional" or how to be more "missional" coming from the emerging church in the East. It's just what and who they are. If you called them missional, they wouldn't know what you're talking about. It's fascinating — we're dissecting the word, developing concepts, forming lectures and teachings on what it is, mapping out plans on how to be "missional," and yet most of us have never even experienced it. This humbles me tremendously as a westerner.

This may be the biggest difference between how we intentionally start churches in the West and how they unintentionally start movements in the East that explode like wildfire.

Even so, many are talking about starting movements here in the West. We fund, plan and strategize our focus on starting something that grows into a movement from a single church. And often we get the growing church — yet not the movement. On the other hand, the believers in the two-thirds world get the movement even though they were not expecting it! The differences in the philosophy, focus, the expected results, and the motive are all reversed! Their philosophy is based more on discipleship where people know who Christ is and follow it together, never expecting big results. People who are focusing on church planting are talking movement language because we've seen it "over there" and want it "here." What would it look

like for us here in the United States to learn from the church in
Vietnam, China, or even Tehran? I wonder.

How Can That Be?

I have a vision and a dream. Let's start a thousand churches over the next
ten years, each one running a minimum of two thousand members, and in
just ten years we will turn America upside down with the gospel! That would
work, right? Wrong—that scenario just happened over the past ten years, and
there are fewer people in church today than ever before. How can that be?
How could we have spent billions to start two thousand megachurches and
yet have fewer people in church and a society that largely feels the church is
antagonistic?

The answer is, in part, that it's not enough just to start churches for the
sake of evangelism that will end when "conversion" takes place. Books on
starting churches generally operate on the premise that we need to start
churches because it is the best evangelistic method that exists. That is a true
statement—but an insufficient reason for starting churches. Any research
regarding the state of church growth and Christianity in America says it is in
decline. Thom Rainer, author and columnist, wrote:

> I am by nature an optimist. I have seen the hand of God too often
> in my life to live in a state of despair and defeatism. However, the
> state of evangelism in the American Church is such that I do have
> my moments when I wonder if the Church is headed down the path
> of many European congregations: decline and death. The facts of a
> 2004 research project I led are sobering.[1]

Regardless of the religious right and despite the emergence of megachurches, postmodern churches, and house churches, nothing has stemmed
the tide of Christianity's slow decline in the West. We continue to decline
while the church is simultaneously exploding in the East as the world has
never known.

Everyone is working on it, however. We are designing systems and templates to see a movement happen in the West. Great systems are emerging.
We feel successful if a denomination, network, or group of churches plants a
few hundred churches—as if we may be on the brink of something. We get
excited if a few hundred people or a few thousand gather to discuss church
planting at conferences—and we should. However, our standards for impact
are incredibly low compared to how churches are multiplying around the
world. Upon examination, the movements that are exploding often have poor

systems, little control, and massive fruit. They defy both logic and explanation. It's almost as if the paradoxical principle is that great resources and systems produce little, while few (if any) resources and systems produce masses. Could there be a correlation?

Not long ago, I sat across the table from an extremely wealthy and successful man who was looking to invest his millions. Church planting was high on his list — he has funded different forms of it for years. However, his question to me was, "Is church planting really working?" My answer was succinct. "Not if we keep planting the same kinds of churches." Our tendency has been to look at the form and model — be it seeker, postmodern, house church, whatever. Rarely have we looked at the core, the essence of what a church really is. The result is that we build buildings or gather people, but to what end? We cannot look at converts alone — we have to ask, "Are the churches we are a part of seeing transformation?"

I was at a meeting with Eric Swanson alongside several Christian world leaders at the Global Learning Community gathering. One man named Layo began to speak and his words blew me away and affected Eric as well.

WHY LAYO IS NOT CELEBRATING FORTY YEARS OF MINISTRY
Blog posted by Eric Swanson

Layo Lieva will not be celebrating 40 years of his ministry's presence in El Salvador. But why? Layo has been in ministry for over 30 years, so he has the long view of ministry in one country. He told us about how, when he was a student, he and his friends would dream of what their country would be like if a third of the people in El Salvador knew Christ. "What if . . . ? grew legs as they began strategizing on reaching their country. Now, 30 years later, 32% of El Salvadorenos are believers, the country has statistically been evangelized at least three-times over and there is one church for every 700 El Salvadorenos. (The Saturation Church Planting folks suggest that one church for every thousand people is saturation.) Christian TV and radio stations abound, missionaries flow freely into the country and visiting Christian dignitaries often visit the country's president to pray with him and have their photo taken. There are Jesus marches replete with banners and bands. Layo notes that there is "a festival of Christian work." By many accounts there is much cause for rejoicing. So why is Layo so discontent? Why is he unwilling to have a celebration of his ministry's 40th anniversary in this country?

Let's take a closer look. Layo says that the mental and moral infrastructure of the country is destroyed. Nine people a day die by violent crimes. Drug use is out of control. 35% of people are unemployed. Gangs are prolific and violent. One study showed that 32% of gang members come from evangelical homes. The most common complaint to the police is "evangelical noise"... preachers who drive through the streets blaring their message from speakers mounted atop their cars. The country is much worse off now than in 1980 when there were only 5% believers.

So what went wrong? Layo gives us his deliberate thought... "We don't need to do better but we do need to do different. I'm not sure if we need any more church plants that are like the ones we have. We need a different kind of church." El Salvador, in some ways, is a laboratory for ministry methods. We can see the end game of simple saturation strategies. We can learn a lot about tactics, strategies but most important "the gospel."

One might conclude from El Salvador that the gospel is not efficacious. But maybe the problem lies not with the gospel, in all its fullness, that Jesus preached and what we have passed off as the gospel. It's not the gospel plus something else, but a matter of unpacking the genuine gospel ... it is about the King and the Kingdom. It's about Ephesians 2:10 as well as Ephesians 2:8, 9. It's about loving one's neighbor as well as loving God. It's about community transformation as well as personal transformation. It's about you ... and about me.

Surprising Discoveries

Why have people started churches throughout history? (Keep in mind this is a purely Western perspective on the reason why.)

We don't have any record of believers starting churches in Jerusalem. What we do know is that they met from house to house and also had large gatherings. The reason the church happened in Jerusalem was to coalesce all the people who became believers, starting from the day of Pentecost forward. In other words, the church in Jerusalem began for a different reason than the one in Antioch. The church in Antioch started churches to transform the world. Likewise, the motivation changed for the church in Constantine's era and thereafter when churches were started to spread Christendom and an empire.

Time/Place		Motivation
Jerusalem	→	Community
Antioch	→	Transformation
310 Constantine	→	Christendom and empire
350–800	→	Evangelization
900	→	Holy Roman Empire
1517	→	Reformation
1800	→	Denominationalism
1970	→	Communication and relevance
2005	→	Living incarnationally locally
2010	→	Global transformation

Figure 1: Why Start Churches?

From AD 340 to 800, churches were started in other lands for evangelization—St. Patrick would be the prototype. In 900, it was about the Holy Roman Empire. In 1517, starting churches was about reforming the church. In the nineteenth century, it was about denominations (a trend that is almost over). In the 1970s, it was about relevance. For the most part, our church planting rationale drove church planting globally until after World War II.

There was a great increase in missionaries after World War II because of soldiers who went to war and saw the world. They planted the seeds for the emergence of the global church that is now coming of age. Their reason for planting churches was not to bring about "incarnation"—that's how they lived.

Today, the reasons why the East plants other churches have to do with every single person getting an opportunity to hear and respond to the good news of Jesus. It's about hope and reconciliation in a developing world that is difficult for many people. So while we are deconstructing church, attempting to remake or reinvent it here out of frustration in order to build it back, they are constructing it there out of excitement, enthusiasm, and hope.

The question as to why we are starting churches is crucial to our future. In the West, many leaders are talking about Church Planting Movements (hereafter referred to as CPMs). It is a term derived by missionaries to describe what they saw occurring in certain places in the world. Immediately we picked up on it in the West and began using the "movement" vocabulary despite the fact that there is no one alive today who has ever seen one. In the United States it's been over 120 years since we've seen a church planting movement.

Much is being written right now about what CPMs are and how they happen, but those writing have not been involved in one. CPMs are a non-North

American phenomenon that we are trying to claim for ourselves (or build templates to accomplish) because we want the effect.

There is no doubt about it—we want a movement. We want to know where we are, where we need to be, and what it will take to get us there. We want to see a movement that will transform societies similar to what has happened in the past and is happening in the East. However, churches that multiply in movements are far more than the Sunday event. This is just one of several discoveries I've been making about movements that I think are key to getting where we want to be.

Discovery 1: It's not about a church planting movement—it's about a Jesus movement!

Five years ago, if you were to visit China and meet one of many pastors with tens of thousands in his church (and some millions of millions in their church network), you might ask him, "How did you start this church planting network? How does it feel to lead something so large and successful?" Surprise—he wouldn't know what you were talking about.

It wasn't as if a Chinese person accepted Christ, followed God's call into the ministry, and then felt led to start a church planting movement. Instead, it happened this way: Individuals found Jesus, he revolutionized their lives, and as a result Jesus spread from their lives to the lives of their family and friends. Then, so many wound up following Jesus that churches were necessary to assimilate all the people. It was a *Jesus movement!*

It is crucial to understand that church planting movements are second-tier movements to Jesus movements.[2] The focus isn't on the church or the bride, but on the bridegroom and the relationship with him.

The Great Awakenings, occurring in the 1700s and 1800s in the United States, always led to an increase in church planting—but church planting did not bring about the Great Awakenings. The Pentecostal Awakening, Azusa Street, would ultimately lead to massive church planting that continues to excel to this day, but it started as a focus on Jesus. The Jesus movement of the 1970s gave birth to Calvary Chapels. Campus Crusade for Christ focused on sharing the gospel and making disciples and has wound up being responsible for the conversion of millions of people and the planting of thousands of churches. The point is that the real movement is a Jesus movement, where the gospel builds momentum, not a church planting movement. I like to talk about "Jesus movements," but because industrialization gave birth to globalization, we rush quickly to the machine.

Our time, effort, energy, and focus must be on how the gospel is spreading and how disciples are being made. If we do that, we will get to the church planting movement. It's a lot easier to build buildings, fill them up, and have special events than it is to pour into the lives of people and make multiplying disciples. But it is the only thing that will really work.

This is crucial to understand because we can artificially inseminate, organize, systematize, and even start new churches, thinking that if we only start enough churches, we will get a movement. At the conclusion of all that, however, people wind up exhausted and depressed, still wondering what's wrong with their machine. Instead, we must place the focus on the "Jesus movement." If we understand this, it will have an impact on what kind of church we plant and how. How we apply this understanding determines what we focus on and what we do.

Jesus movements are about Jesus. They're not about the church or the ministry or our success in the ministry. No amount of human trivial religious success can come close to comparing to the glory of God and the wonder of Jesus. It is about Jesus living present and at home within us and moving powerfully through us. The focus of a Jesus movement is not technique but intimacy with the living God.

David Garrison, author of *Church Planting Movements*, references David Watson, who has worked globally and been involved in some of the greatest church planting movements in the world (past and present). I interviewed Watson to help shed some light on the difference between a church planting movement and a Jesus movement. When I asked him if he thought I was off base on this, he said, "Do you know how the term 'church planting movements' came about?" Watson then shared about being at the table with a group of other missionaries when the term crystallized. They were trying to describe what they were seeing take place in the East. "It was never meant to be the key. It was descriptive," he told me.

Watson went on to say, "CPMs are our hope and prayer. Our part of that is making disciples, equipping leaders, and starting churches with the right DNA that is based on obedience. God's part is blessing our obedience in his time with the rapid and regular multiplication of disciples, leaders, and churches." Watson likes the term "gospel planting" because we plant the gospel and train obedience and the result is churches. The focus is not on the act of church planting itself.

The Jesus movement is an intense personal relationship with Jesus. Upon close inspection, most Jesus movements don't come from revival meetings, tract distribution, preaching crusades, mass evangelism campaigns, and "evangelistic" strategies. The key is that someone becomes a follower of Jesus and his power is transformational in their lives. They find this so attractive that others want it. While I believe in the house church movement in America and want to see it succeed, I get concerned when middle-aged, frustrated people all of a sudden want to opt into house churches because they're frustrated with existing churches.

Frustrated people generally don't start movements — but sometimes they do start wars! People who start house churches in America often do so because they want a different kind of church and experience. People in house churches globally don't think of themselves as house churches; they just see themselves as churches. They're excited about Jesus and he is transforming their lives. Other people get involved because they see transformation taking place, and so on.

The comparison is easy to see: one group goes to a house church because they're frustrated with what is; another group goes to a house church because they're excited about the change taking place in someone's life. If the house church is going to become a movement in the United States, and I want that, it will come from young people who are excited about Jesus and want to follow him out of obedience instead of frustration.

Discovery 2: Jesus movements are highly personal and highly societal.

That mix is explosive. These movements are relational with an organic quality to them where social networks become the mode of travel. This means they are viral and travel wherever Jesus followers go. Wherever the gospel has its most transformative impact in someone's life, it directly affects everyone around that person. This obviously leads to the natural evangelization of family and friends. Missiologists have helped us better understand this concept through observing the New Testament "household" conversions such as the Philippian jailer's and others. Had not whole households been affected, the gospel would not have spread like it did. Had it only resulted in isolated individual conversions, it never could have gained the same traction. David Watson has challenged me to envision not just an individual conversion, but a family or relational network of conversions.

As people became followers of Jesus in the early church, he specifically changed their ethics, morality, and views on eternity, which had a huge impact on how they cared for others in society. As followers of Jesus, they understood that they were to love, serve, and obey God. Consequently, as Rodney Stark in his brilliant book *The Rise of Christianity* writes, "Cyprian, Dionysius, Eusebius, and other church fathers thought the epidemics made major contributions to the Christian cause."[3] Dionysius wrote in his Easter letter that Christian values of love and charity had been, from the beginning, translated into norms of social service and community solidarity. Thus, when disaster struck, the Christians wound up with higher rates of survival because they took care of each other. Stark writes, "The contents of Christian and pagan beliefs were different in ways that greatly determined not only their explanatory capacities but also their relative capacities to mobilize human resources."[4]

Following each epidemic, Christians comprised a larger percentage of the population, even without converts! Their higher survival rates were a statement to Christians and non-Christians alike and also prompted pagans to shift to Christian social networks.

The gospel spread in social networks not only because of the observable change in the lives of its followers, but also because of the attractive nature of a Christian philosophy of life. Whereas in Roman culture people were the pawns of the gods, in Christianity there was a beginning and an end—an eternity, a hope in the midst of suffering and even death. Dionysius wrote:

> Most of our brother Christians showed unabounded love and loyalty, never sparing themselves and thinking only of one another. Heedless of danger, they took charge of the sick, attending to their every need and ministering to them in Christ, and with them departed this life serenely happy; for they were infected by others with the disease.... The best of our brothers lost their lives in this manner ... death in this form ... seems in every way the equal of martyrdom.[5]

Emperor Julian, who tried to bring back the old Roman gods, launched a campaign to institute pagan charities in order to match the Christians. "Julian complained in a letter to the high priest of Galatia in 362 that the pagans needed to equal the virtues of Christians, for recent Christian growth was caused by their 'moral character, even if pretended' ... 'they support not only their poor, but ours as well, everyone can see that our people lack aid from us.' "[6]

The social networks obviously found footing in the urban centers. Max Weber, the German sociologist, thought it "highly improbable" that Christianity could have developed as it did outside of an urban setting.[7] Matthew's gospel, which was considered by some to be the most popular for the early church, is said to have been written in the fourth largest urban center, Antioch. The cities were small and people were crammed on top and beside one another. It was common in Rome for buildings to collapse suddenly from the weight.

In Rome, there was one private house for every twenty-six blocks of apartments. According to Stark, "tenants rarely had more than one room in which entire families were herded together."[8] People living this close together, facing illness and invaders, no doubt had a grapevine of communication that was incredibly viral. Those difficult living conditions were exceptionally ripe for the spread of the gospel. All of this proved to be a huge lesson for me about how planting the gospel should always start with the society and not the church.

Discovery 3: Jesus movements take time.

As I began to study and connect globally with movements, I initially interpreted them in terms of what I saw at that moment. One of my biggest mistakes early on was the failure to recognize years of work others had done to see that a movement got to the place where it was. Jesus movements don't happen as quickly as people often think they do. Foolishly and in ignorance I used to say, "When the missionaries were thrown out of China—that's when the gospel spread like wildfire" — the idea being that nothing happened until 1947. That isn't true. Hudson Taylor, Robert Morrison, and others labored there 150 years earlier. The seeds have to be planted for the movement to gain momentum. It took the early church 350 years to get to movement status. In the United States, the greatest church planting period came in the 1800s, 200 years after the pilgrims landed.

We have a rather skewed view of movements and we confuse them with fads, trends, and hype. Legitimate Jesus movements are not like Beanie Babies — two-dollar cloth dolls that eventually sold for hundreds of dollars (only to be worth fifty cents today — yes, I bought a couple)! Jesus movements keep their value like hundred-year-old Hummels. Many people who want a movement have read *The Tipping Point* by Malcolm Gladwell.[9] I like the book and have learned much from it. However, frankly, *Good to Great* by Jim Collins[10] may be a more accurate approach because it doesn't track merely the sale of a product like Hush Puppy shoes, but it takes a long look at corporations and how they grow over decades and centuries. This is what movements are really like — where Christianity brings about massive change.

When we see something happen like what we are seeing in China today, where the curve is now exponential, we want it. But we can't ignore that people had been planting seeds for centuries before that movement came. Let me illustrate using China as an example (see Figure 2). The process of planting the gospel seed appears to be about two hundred years. Next, there is a progression from the exponential growth of a Jesus movement that leads to new churches being planted (in this case, house churches in China in the 1960s). From there it becomes a full-fledged CPM, then church multiplication, then the institution (the larger the institution, the less the planting). After that there are movements, but not massive national movements or people group movements. Only movements within existing movements.

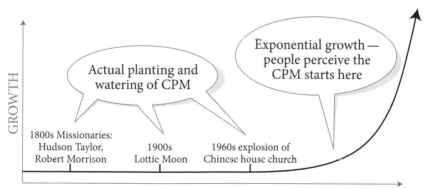

Figure 2: Movement Continuum

If the early seeds of the gospel don't take root, it will never lead to a movement. Roman Catholic missionaries went to Japan in the 1400s, and Christianity began to flourish quickly. An emperor came to power who was vehemently opposed to this sudden rise in Christianity. So he crucified Christians at low tide in the ocean and literally wiped Christianity off the map in Japan. It has stayed off the map.

All of us are somewhere on that movement continuum. However, regardless of where we are, we must be faithful, whether we are a pioneer on the front end trekking over difficult mountains or a surfer on the exponential curve experiencing the thrills of the wave.

Outside of Christianity, civil rights and a woman's right to vote are movements that remind us that movements take time, and we must not grow discouraged. We shiver when we read reports that faith is "gone" in a generation. We should work hard, wisely, and quickly, but we should never forget God is in control in a much bigger picture.

Discovery 4: Jesus movements are led by disciples, not by church planters.

The lowest common denominator is not a pastor, planter, or prophet — but the disciple. Spreading the gospel isn't dependent on a building, a pulpit, a speaker, or an organization. If a church has those things, they should exist to facilitate the discipleship focus. When people hear the word "discipleship," they often grow exhausted just thinking about it. To them, it means lots of education and lots of training and programs, but often little impact.[11]

However, consider the story of a man I met on the other side of the world whose only encounter with the gospel came through a radio transmission of a Bible program. I had heard about this exceptional young man who had started dozens of churches, and I couldn't wait to meet him. When we entered his village, I began looking for this amazing leader. To my surprise, he came walking out of a nearby field: barefoot, very small, and very young. He was only twenty years old and told me his story.

At age sixteen, he happened to hear the story of Christ on a radio program. In faith, he made a decision in the middle of his house, in the middle of a field, to give his heart to Christ. He began to live his faith in a radical way, witnessing to all of his friends, who eventually organized into a worship community. Things became difficult for him, resulting in several years of hardship and persecution. However, he stayed firm and consistent. In four or five years, having no formal training or seminary (his only copy of Scripture was not even in his native tongue), this young man became a part of the planting of more churches in his part of the world than any American pastor in the United States has ever seen.

The gospel has never been dependent on great preachers — but on great lives and unknown names that would die with people in an ancient plague or in a modern crisis.

Discovery 5: Historically, there is only one national Jesus movement per nation that involves everyone. After that, there are submovements within the broader movement.

This is an observation that I hope is proven false, but I have not yet found the exception. When the Christian faith was first introduced to the Roman empire, it grew and then became a mighty torrent that flooded the culture. After its first movement, there were submovements and stories about God's using people, but never in the same way as the initial movement. Modern Europe has seen the same phenomenon. In the areas where the Celtic church exploded, it never grew at the same pace as that initial burst, although other great things ensued. In the United States from the mid-1800s to the mid-1900s, the church grew as it never had before — or has since.

There is no way you can minimize what God has done in America over the past one hundred years. The difference is that the impact after that initial burst began to be felt more outside America than inside. The rise of the global missionary movement from the 1900s to the mid-1960s has had a profound impact on the world. The Azusa Street revival and the birth of Pentecostalism was a movement within the broader movement that reshaped some of American Christianity. Its greatest gift proved to be how it would impact the world. Youth With A Mission — founded by Loren Cunningham — has mobilized millions of young people and adults alike to engage every nation on the globe, alongside Bill Bright and Campus Crusade for Christ.

This is becoming the story of Korea, too. The resources, systems, processes, and institutions were put in place for the Korean Christians to reach out, and they are now like no other nation on the face of the earth. Some people believe the soul of Christianity is now in Seoul. However, as I speak to Korean pastors, they are concerned that there is not the same passion for Jesus in Korea that there was just twenty years ago.

I think it's a God thing. He wants his gospel taken to every tongue, tribe, and nation. He moves on people and sends his Spirit; the result is that movements are born that outstrip any system or process. Once the church is in place and begins to mature, we act as partners in reconciliation to coalesce our resources and people to touch the world. We see cooperation like never before as churches go after something bigger than us — the world. It is what Alan Hirsch calls the "missional impulse" or simply the forward motion of the faith.

This is where things get messy. I used to think institutions were bad; they aren't. Imagine a society without government, police protection, universities, hospitals, or churches. Institutions are the stories of people who were once a movement and (hopefully) continue to hold the historic values of a society in check. The problem is that the institutions are driven more by the past and outdated methodology. If we don't change with the present, personal agendas come into play—and we get into trouble. You can follow the movement of the church and the movement of the gospel in similar patterns (see Figure 3).

Movement of the Church:

Jerusalem →
  Antioch →
    Constantinople →
      Rome →
        London/Paris/Geneva/Wittenberg/ →
        North America →
        Korea →
          China →? (I think India)

How the Gospel Engages Nations:

Gospel →
  Disciple →
    Society →
      Movement →
        Church →
          Multiplication →
          Institution →
          Reformation

Figure 3: Movement of the Church vs. How the Gospel Engages Nations

In the second example of how the gospel engages nations, the gospel is planted and a disciple is born. Numerous disciples begin to impact society. A movement begins. The church grows and multiplies. This leads to the organization of the movement, which forms the first steps toward the birth of an institution. The institution reforms or dies over the years.

Discovery 6: Jesus movements surge from the young.

This means, at least for us in the West, that the most important ministry and focus in our local churches *must* be our youth ministry. Ever wonder why the best pastors and church planters are often former youth ministers? Jonathan Edwards was central in the preacher role of the First Great Awakening in America; however, it was a movement that began among young people and was driven by young people. He produced many David Brainerds with a contagious enthusiasm for the Lord.

Brainerd, orphaned by the age of fourteen, converted to Christ during his first year at Yale. He became a missionary to the Indians and was engaged to Jonathan Edwards' daughter. However, he fell ill and returned home to Edwards' house to die at age twenty-nine. He had kept a journal, published by Edwards two years after Brainerd's death, that records his experiences as a missionary and his spiritual reflections on his calling—a work that has inspired countless other young missionaries.

Those of us who are old enough and have gained enough credibility to lead the institutions, handle resources, and become voices in the faith community must not focus merely on building the church for our generation but on extending the church to future generations. That means we keep our core but release our language, music, and methods. Emerging churches must hold on to truth in their core, but communicate to and be shaped by emerging generations. Failing to do so is why the church has become empty around the world.

Old men and women play a crucial role in the future church; it isn't to hold on to the forms, but to hold on to a personal Jesus movement in their hearts so that young people can say of old people, "Oh man, I want to know Jesus like they know Jesus." It is not, "I want to do church like they do church." The only way that will work is for old folks to pour themselves into young hearts and mentor and love them so much that they would die for them. When that happens, you become more concerned about our youth than you do your tight grip.

I will always be grateful to Leighton Ford for playing this role in my life. He has been my "old man" even before he was sixty! That is why I make no major decision without calling him first—even to this day. Presbyterian like Leighton? No. Loving Jesus and living for him like Leighton? I can only hope.

Discovery 7: Jesus movements are collaborative.

No single denomination, person, network, or model has ever started a movement. This is why I've come to dislike labels and brands. Only when everyone dies to themselves and everyone comes together do we see Jesus. For a movement to gain momentum, we have to focus on the core of what it is. For us, it's Jesus.

In China, the movement has involved everyone. Sadly, in the past ten years, as denominations and organizations from the West have shown up to "help," their presence has had a divisive effect on the church in China. I've seen the same thing in other parts of the world. I see fresh expressions of God working globally, and candidly I fear what we in the West might do if we think we are going to run over and "save them" or help them. They are doing just fine with the Spirit. We need to leave them alone, except to sit at their feet to learn, which means the only talking we do is to ask questions.

Discovery 8: Jesus movements hinge on the Holy Spirit.

A Jesus movement goes beyond our planning and execution. It goes beyond our ability. Only the Spirit can take a horrible plague and cause it to be an opportunity for Christians to show the love of Jesus. Unavoidable tragedy is our opportunity for the world to see Jesus at work. The Spirit takes a tragedy like a tsunami or an earthquake and turns it into an eternal hope. If a human being stirs it up, it soon fizzles. If the Spirit stirs it up—get out of the way and mount your surfboard! This is what I call the missiology of grabbing what is in front of your face, seeing what the Spirit is up to, and living faith in the moment.

Recently we had a huge baptismal service in our church. As each person entered the baptistery, we read their story. One young lady accepted Christ on September 11, 2001. I couldn't believe it — it stopped me in my tracks; that tragedy turned her to God. I looked out at the congregation, shook my head, and said, "Thank you, bin Laden — Jesus wins!"

One Exciting Proposition

Based on these last few discoveries, those here in America may get the idea that we don't have much of a role to play in the future beyond giving our money and support. It looks as if we have to sit on the sidelines and watch everyone play ball at a higher level.

However, remember there is one community that we are all a part of that has yet to experience a Jesus movement — the entire world. We are a part of that. If you had the choice of living in the first Great Awakening with Jonathan Edwards or being part of the potential emerging first Global Great Awakening, which would you choose? Why be just one nation when you could be part of a global movement?

The movement is globally expansive but not yet strategically connected. That's where we come in. Think of what we have to offer the rest of the world: wealth, pragmatism, systems, industry, and technology. If we give these things sacrificially and in humility to the world as the early Christians did in serving Europe during the plagues, they could be the glue, tracks, and web that everyone can use to see the emergence of the world's first global Jesus movement. That would then lead to the world's first global church planting movement.

What better time to be alive? What more exciting faith adventure and movement could you be a part of than this one? Welcome to twenty-first-century Christianity — alas, a Texas-sized vision!

The New Math

$$CPM - CP + J = JM$$

A church planting movement (CPM) minus church planting (CP) leaves a movement. But what kind of movement do we want? Add to that Jesus (J) and you get what we are all after — a Jesus movement (JM).

Chapter 2

COMING SOON— THE FIRST GLOBAL CHURCH PLANTING MOVEMENT

JM x C + NT = CPM

I'm not the only one thinking about a global Church Planting Movement. The Chinese are the first not only to dream of a global CPM, but also to act on it. They have a focus called the "Back to Jerusalem Movement," in which their stated goal is to plant churches all along the Silk Road back to Jerusalem.

I remember the first time I met a Chinese pastor. I thought he would like to talk about the success behind his house church network, which happens to be several tens of thousands strong. Instead, he spent the next few minutes telling me what I didn't expect to hear. He wasn't impressed with his own network; rather, he was a man obsessed with the whole world. His eyes gleamed when he shared his longing for opportunities that his network of tens of thousands could use to engage billions worldwide.

Not long after that I read *The Heavenly Man*, about a Chinese church planter named Pastor Yun who has seen thousands of people come to Christ in China.[1] He, too, is part of this movement. God keeps bringing people across my path with this same global vision. During a recent trip to Hong Kong, I met another Chinese pastor who has lived with a dream of a global CPM. We talked that day and emailed several times afterward about what it would be like to engage the whole world. I'll never forget his earnestness and passion when he said, "I'm tired of going to conferences where people present papers about this stuff. I just want to do it."

For the first time in many centuries, the church in the West sees something in the East that she wants, and furthermore, that she didn't start! We must be honest about this; we have not had recent church planting movements in the West. In America, it hasn't happened since the 1800s, and it has been centuries since the last one in Europe. It is an Eastern description of the activity of the church—not a goal, dream, or plan, but an activity presently taking place.

A Picture of Church

Before we can talk about multiplying churches in a global movement, we must know what it is that we are multiplying. What is the church? In my tradition, the short definition I was taught was "a baptized body of believers." That falls woefully short and could make me one and the same with a group of Mormons or any other religion/cult that practices baptism. I've learned that many different authors, theologians, and pastors define the church in many ways (see Figure 4).

Core definition	Key characteristics	Key functions
"The community of all true believers for all time"[2]	• Visible and invisible • Local and universal[3]	• Ministry to God in worship • Ministry to believers • Ministry to the world[4]
"The community of the Kingdom"[5]	• Not the same as the Kingdom, but created out of the Kingdom • Instrument of the Kingdom • Custodian of the Kingdom[6]	• Preach the good news (of the Kingdom, not the church) • Human fellowship • Witness to the Kingdom • Minister through the Holy Spirit[7]
"A covenanted community—centered on Jesus"[8]	• Enjoying a distinctive bond • Participating in salvation • Receiving God's grace in Christ[9]	• Worship • Discipleship • Mission[10]

Figure 4: What Is the Church?

Alan Hirsch, author of *The Forgotten Ways*, reminds us that we need to spend some time thinking about the definition of the church because we're often so close to it that we can't see it for what it is and what it is supposed to be.

December 29
Blog posted by Alan Hirsch

For many of us, church has been something we have lived with and around for much of our lives. And this is a good thing because the community of faith is meant to be a living community of God's people. But the problem is that hanging around it for so long, we get to assume that we actually know what it is — what exactly makes it the church. Having been in it for such a long time actually makes it increasingly hard to "see" and therefore define. Kinda like a fish trying to describe the water it swims in. But getting to grips with missionality and missional church requires that we first get to grips with what the *ecclesia* really *is*.

So coming out of my own story, and assuming the role of the Spirit and the Bible (because without these you cannot even know Jesus truly) I came up with the following functional 'definition' of what *ecclesia* is comprised of.

A church is....

A covenanted community: A church is formed people not by people just hanging out together, but ones bound together in a distinctive bond. There is a certain obligation toward one another formed around a covenant.

Centered on Jesus: He is the new covenant with God and he thus forms as the true epicenter of an authentic Christian faith.[11] An *ecclesia* is not just a God-community — there are many such religious communities around. We are defined by our relationship to the second person of the Trinity, the Mediator, Jesus Christ. A covenant community centered around Jesus participates in the salvation that he brings. We receive the grace of God in Him. But, more is required to truly constitute a church...

A true encounter with God in Jesus must result in:

- Worship; defined as offering our lives back to God through Jesus.
- Discipleship; defined as following Jesus and becoming increasingly like him (Christlikeness).

- Mission; defined as extending the mission (the redemptive purposes) of God through the activities of his people.

It needs to be noted that in practice, as well as theologically, these are profoundly inter-linked and inform each other to create a complex phenomenon called 'church.'

This definition is important for me because it distills the core aspects of what constitutes a faith *ecclesia*.

So what's in a definition? Actually the way we define church is crucial because it gives us a direct clue to the critical elements of authentic Christian community. It also highlights for us the major responses that constitute Christian spirituality, namely worship, discipleship, and mission. We will be weighed up by God on the basis of the innate purpose of the church and thus our capacity to:

1. Center our common life on Jesus
2. Cultivate covenant community
3. Make disciples: people who are learning how, and what it means, to become Christlike
4. Engage in his mission to the world: which is our mission (his purposes flow through us)
5. The authenticity, depth and breadth, of our worship

If we are not fruitful in these areas we cannot claim to be a faithful church as God intended us to be. So the definition serves as a test of fruitfulness and a guide to the kind of activities we need to pursue to remain true to our calling as God's people.

I love Alan's definition because it leads to how the church functions. That same description of the church that he and the other authors give is the same one that's being given over and over again. I don't think I can improve upon it.

Not into Buildings

As people discuss how to do church today, it still rests upon the issue of "place," whether it's in a church building, a house, a storefront, or a coffeehouse. I believe the biggest revolution in "church" for the future is not going to be where she meets but how she operates and how she is dispersed. Joel Hunter pastors the aptly named church in Orlando, Florida — The Church Distributed. Laypeople (or nonpreachers) are not into buildings — they're more into engagement. Doing church is the church engaging the community and the world around it.

Another example is Chris Seiple, president of the Institute for Global Engagement. He works worldwide through this organization in areas of human rights and religious freedom. IGE describes itself as a "think-tank with legs." Seiple works with numerous state departments both here in the United States and around the world.[12] Chris is a unique person—the combination of a Marine and a classically trained diplomat with a PhD from Tufts University. Some recent back-and-forth emails between him and me give you a sense of his idea of church.

> My use of "apostolic"—to my current and emerging understanding—is threefold. Obviously it's a reference back to the original intent for the church, the church undivided. Second it is a reference to the need for apostles back in the Church in America to inspire and equip American Christians to catch up with the global Church, to catch up with God's sovereignty and what He's already doing in the world ... that is, to finally break the back of this old evangelical paradigm that fixates on the harvest but forgets how to water ... Third, the Church was designed to be the holistic missionary, transforming society from within. It is not merely a structure that administers the sacraments through theologically trained people; it is bigger than a building because His Church is "God's House."[13]
>
> If we are His house and not defined by the building, then we are all missionaries, any vocation, any location. IGE is the church. So is Wycliffe. And thus we need disciples who have been equipped as ambassadors.[14] Our state is the Kingdom and our interest is to advance it by loving our neighbor ... through our understanding of politics and culture—[so that] our neighbor understands (or it is not love) ... and the only way to do that is to serve as salt across all society's sectors ... this is the Church transforming the local culture from within.
>
> Chris Seiple

In another email:

> I would say the Church is a way of life, a mindset and a methodology ... a significant part of which is the actual building and bills ... the sacraments are the center, of course, but you do not need a building to do that. This understanding would be my definition of radical incarnation.

I agree that "para" should be dropped from the lexicon. In my understanding of the church, we are different members of the same body, trying actively to act more often as one — as mutually reinforcing elements — reinvigorating the church building and its community by dismembering its usual inward focus.

"All authority in heaven and on earth has been given to me." I take this verse to mean that God is already there, working in all sectors of society — in ways beyond our imagination, in ways that are His and will never be ours — to call the people of that society back to Himself. I also believe that as Kingdom ambassadors, our job is to indeed "plead"[15] for Him, such that people are reconciled to Him ... put differently, our job is to find ways to appeal to the local context such that we can plead. We can only do this if we are daily transformed by the decision to actively know Jesus better today than we did yesterday. If you accept the notion that individuals make up nations and that nations make up societies, then there is a call to transform societies from within as His already present House.

Chris Seiple

Chris sees "church" in what he does. This is a massive and healthy shift. Get ready, church leaders of all models; these people do not want to be led in the same way that "church members" are led today—but that's what my next book is about!

CPMS — Not What You Think

Now that we have defined the church, the next question we must answer is this: "What is a church planting movement, and what is its role in the larger Jesus movement?" In the expansion of Christianity, nothing comes close in comparison—in terms of having the potential to change the culture—like that of a church planting movement, so we'd better understand it.

No one gives us a better definition than David Garrison in his book *Church Planting Movements.*[16] Garrison helps us understand that church planting movements are not revivals, mass evangelism, people movements, or church growth, nor are they just a miracle. There is something of a path. Finally, I know this guy gets it because he makes it clear they are not an end in themselves. A church planting movement is not an event; it isn't a program; and it has a totally different way of measuring metrics.

A Church Planting Movement is not a ...	A Church Planting Movement is ...

• revival
• people movement
• church growth
• miracle
• event
• program
	"a rapid multiplication of indigenous churches planting churches that sweeps through a people group or population segment." (David Garrison, *Church Planting Movements*)
	
	Key words:
	  • rapid
	  • multiplication
	  • indigenous
	  • churches planting churches
	  • people group/population segment

Figure 5: What Is a Church Planting Movement?

Garrison defines a church planting movement as a "rapid multiplication of indigenous churches planting churches that sweeps through a people group or population segment."[17] I've had the privilege of knowing many of the people he writes about in his book and even being near some of them and the movements they were a part of when their movements were just emerging. It has had a profound effect on my own understanding of what that might look like here in the States.

Let's take apart his definition. First, *rapidly reproducing* means the process is faster than you think. In other words, it is almost if not out of control.

Second, *multiplication* means it is not simple addition. Addition movements mean we start one church at a time or even perhaps in a group. The difference in multiplication is that churches wind up starting others that start others. Starting one church a year, ten churches a year, or even a hundred churches a year does not mean movement. Movement is a reality only when those churches that you are planting in turn wind up planting other churches (see Figure 6).

Addition is linear. It is one church after the other, after the other.

Multiplication is wildfire. It is an unpredictable pattern.

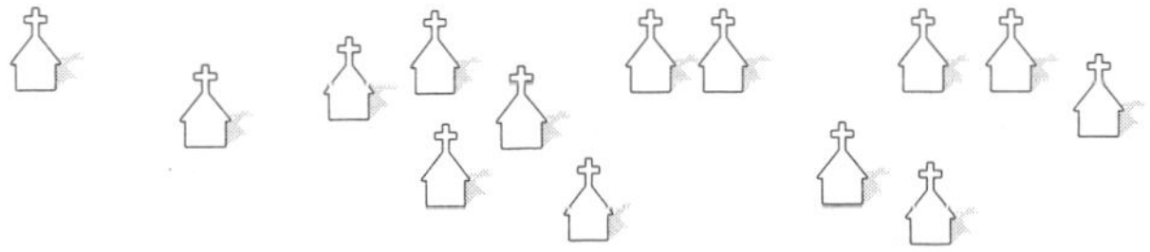

Figure 6: Church Addition Compared to Church Multiplication

The third word in this definition is *indigenous*—meaning generated from within, as opposed to being started by outsiders. This is the idea that the adherents are propelling the movement, not just the leaders. There are times when movements are begun by an outsider; they are rare. Even so, if the nationals are not driving it within a short period of time, then there is the real possibility—if not reality—that it will never become a movement.

Not long ago, Eddy Leo from Abba Love Church in Jakarta, Indonesia, spoke at our church. His story blew us all away. Eddy now has 25,000 people involved in his church. How did that happen? It started when he found Jesus and, along with two other guys, led his college friends to the Lord. From this tiny start, that group grew into one of the more significant churches in the entire world. Movements mean ownership and involvement. Movements cannot be orchestrated or driven from the outside—they are movements, not programs.

The fourth characteristic is *churches planting churches*. Though church planters may start the first churches, at some point the churches get into the act. In the United States today when we think of church planting, the focus is on how organizations and denominations recruit the very best church planters. Our current focus on the use of "professional pastors" almost ensures that we will not get to church planting movements.

This is what the house church movement has to teach the broader church community in the United States. Some of the best church planters have been businessmen, lawyers, and those from a thousand other vocations. Churches have to own church planting, and that means giving it to the people. It has to be viewed as seriously as any other ministry in the church, if not the core of what it means to see radical transformation in communities, nations, and the world. There are no church planting movements that emerged from denominations, networks, or alliances—all of them have come from local churches that were multiplying like crazy. It's a lot easier to develop an organization than it is to make the church produce—but once it starts, it's next to impossible to stop.

Fifth, Garrison notes the context of a CPM as *people groups or interrelated population segments*. This will be the biggest challenge in seeing a global church planting movement. Ultimately, I believe there may be several if not hundreds of thousands of church planting movements that are global in nature. Just starting a church overseas doesn't make a movement a global church planting movement.

Why a Global Church Planting Movement Makes Sense

A global church planting movement is the natural progression from where we have come. Looking for a church planting movement in a Third World country is far easier than trying to find one or even see one emerge in the United States or the Western world. To some, the mere desire to see a global church planting movement would seem impossible enough. But not really. What is there left to do after national and indigenous church planting movements? I believe a global church planting movement is the next natural progression.

Twenty years ago when I started NorthWood in Texas there weren't a lot of people wanting to start churches—especially the more gifted people. Now there are many. To many, church planting is becoming the "pastorate of choice" as opposed to taking some existing church filled with other people's headaches! Now, when I hear young pastors talk, they are all talking about wanting to start church planting movements.

Yet most don't really understand what that means. They feel as if they can create a movement or drive it as they do a single local church. Others have the idea that they will start a movement from a church just like theirs. Though some of their ideas may not be entirely spot on, their vision is changing and they are beginning to see that it isn't just about *their* church but about *his* church. I'm hoping that the next generation of church leaders, planters, and disciples will be more obsessed with the global nature of the church and global church planting movements than any generation from the United States heretofore. I may be writing for a young emerging generation!

A global church planting movement is the natural response of the emerging global church. Movements are emerging from other nations to reach other nations. The Chinese, the Brazilians, the Filipinos, the Indonesians, the Mexicans—all are now sending their own missionaries and engaging the world. Why does the church as it emerges and matures globally move forward to other nations and places in the world as never before? Because we all possess the same mission. Isn't it fascinating that as nations begin to figure this out for themselves, they naturally move forward? This is what Jesus described in Acts 1:8: "You will receive power when the Holy Spirit comes on you; and you will be my witnesses in Jerusalem, and in all Judea and Samaria, and to the ends of the earth."

It is also why a global church planting movement will be necessary for every tongue, tribe, and nation. Revelation 5:9–10 says:

> They sang a new song:
> "You are worthy to take the scroll
>   and to open its seals,
> because you were slain,
>   and with your blood you purchased men for God
>   from every tribe and language and people and nation.
> You have made them to be a kingdom and priests to serve our God,
>   and they will reign on the earth."

A global church planting movement will be necessary for the bride of Christ to be prepared for the coming of Christ. I believe a global church planting movement is in line with the church being the bride of Christ and being ready for when Christ returns. The job of the bride is to get herself together and to gather all those who are a part of the body:

> The bride belongs to the bridegroom. The friend who attends the bridegroom waits and listens for him, and is full of joy when he hears the bridegroom's voice. That joy is mine, and it is now complete. He must become greater; I must become less. (John 3:29–30)

> I saw the Holy City, the new Jerusalem, coming down out of heaven from God, prepared as a bride beautifully dressed for her husband. And I heard a loud voice from the throne saying, "Now the dwelling of God is with men, and he will live with them. They will be his people, and God himself will be with them and be their God." (Revelation 21:2–3)

A global church planting movement is possible in a world with an emerging third culture. The biggest challenge to a global church planting movement in Garrison's definition is defining a global indigenous culture. What is the global people group or population segment? Sociologists write about third culture children and this new emerging global culture. Or could it be truly global and not limited to one "flat" population group such as third culture kids?

For example, China will soon be the largest English-speaking nation in the world, trumping the current number one nation of India, where 350 million people speak English! Chinglish is the new designation of new mixes of language. Regardless of what it looks like or what language(s) it incorporates, when the world is won for Christ, a global church planting movement will be connected.

A global church planting movement is possible like never before because of the technology that exists in the world today. With the rise of the Internet, travel, and communication, it won't be difficult to see it happen. It's just a matter of time. I think we'll see the emergence of these movements in the next five to ten years, and I believe they will be fully blown in the next fifteen to twenty-five years.

A global church planting movement will happen only when we learn to treat each other with respect and have a classless and raceless church. This is the point Paul was making when he wrote Galatians 3:26–29:

> You are all sons of God through faith in Christ Jesus, for all of you who were baptized into Christ have clothed yourselves with Christ. There is neither Jew nor Greek, slave nor free, male nor female, for you are all one in Christ Jesus. If you belong to Christ, then you are Abraham's seed, and heirs according to the promise.

Examples of emerging classless, raceless churches today include Newsong Community Church in Irvine, California, where Dave Gibbons is pastor; Erwin McManus's Mosaic; and Brooklyn Tabernacle. The most vibrant example of a raceless, classless church that I've ever experienced is Times Square Church in the heart of Manhattan, started by David Wilkerson.

The early church did experience a global movement. It initially came primarily from Jews, but then it crossed the national boundaries of Israel. Then it crossed races and finally continents. Not only did the early church experience a church planting movement, but one that was global in scope from the very beginning. It seems these days as if everything we are discovering was already present in the early church. How did they do it? There are a couple of clues in the Jerusalem Council in Acts and in the way the Jews decided to respond to the Gentiles.

We have much to learn from each other. To think that all learning is coming from one direction is absurd — especially in the world we live in today. However, we have more to learn from the church in the East than the church in the West has to teach the church in the East. Those of us in the West cannot treat the church in the East as weak and frail — she is much more alive than us. We cannot view her as inferior or as second class.

A global church planting movement will happen only when we recognize there is only one church. Ephesians 4:2 – 6 reminds us:

> Be completely humble and gentle; be patient, bearing with one another in love. Make every effort to keep the unity of the Spirit through the bond of peace. There is one body and one Spirit — just as you were called to one hope when you were called — one Lord, one faith, one baptism; one God and Father of all, who is over all and through all and in all.

There is the church in Africa, but not the African Church. There is the church in the United States, but not the United States Church. There is the church in England, but not the English Church. Christ is the Head of the church, and like it or not — realize it or not — when we accept Christ, all of us are part of an organic church where Jesus is the Head. Churches may be started organically or otherwise. However, one thing is for certain — if it is his church — it is an organic relationship.

"Starting Lots of Churches" and Other False Assumptions

Since church planting movements are a thing of the Spirit, there are some people who will not be a part for sure. Who are they?

- Loudmouths making proclamations of "Here is the way" or "The end has come"
- Frustrated denominational or organizational executives

- Superstar senior pastors
- Self-serving model gurus
- Contemporary, "attraction" guys who make the church a supermarket
- Angry, white house, church guys who are defined more by what they aren't than what they are

There will be a new ethic of humility, collaboration, shared leadership, unity, and cooperation. There are other exceptions and differences that set a global church planting movement apart. What would have to be different from a typical church planting movement (if there is any such thing) in one nation in order to encompass many nations (see Figure 7)?

Call	→	to God
Purpose	→	Glory of God
Vision	→	Global Transformation
Context	→	Society
Theology	→	The Kingdom
System	→	Decentralized
Ethos	→	Multiplication
Organization	→	Relational
Resources	→	Home grown

Our Vision encompasses the whole world. The Context in which we focus is society at large, not the church itself. Our Theology of the Kingdom must be prevalent. The System we use must decentralize. Our Ethos and passion must be for multiplication, not simply linear addition of churches. Our Organization is viral and relational, as it was in the early church. Our Resources are not hired staff; they are home grown.

Figure 7: Scope of a Global Church Planting Movement

Since a church planting movement is a thing of the Spirit and not something we can force, what other things can we do to create the right atmosphere? We know we will have to challenge our old way of doing church and starting churches. We will also have to get over some false assumptions:

	False assumption	**Response**
1	You create a church planting movement by starting a lot of churches.	They must be the right kind of churches.
2	The end game is to plant as many churches as you can.	Only transformational churches will matter.

3	If we reach a lot of seekers, we'll change our community.	For too long we've seen that we can baptize a lot of people and yet see little change.
4	We only need to plant large churches if we want a church planting movement.	Church planting movements are from smaller churches, not megachurches.
5	Networks, organizations, and denominations will start church planting movements if they just come together.	There must be freedom of form and ministry for it to happen.
6	If we get a lot of people showing up on Sunday, we'll get a church planting movement.	We've been doing this for years in the U.S. and we haven't seen that happen. There must be intentionality.
7	We are starting churches to reach the lost; that is what drives a church planting movement.	Evangelism is only one function of church planting churches.

It Can and Will Happen

There wasn't much written about church planting movements just ten years ago. Even so, many pastors, organizations, and groups are talking about "starting their own church planting movements"—as if they can just jump-start it and make it happen. Many feel that if they get their processes in place and start a few churches, they are at movement status. I'm not sure they totally understand what the movement has been around the world, but at least they've caught a glimpse of something bigger. We're often too quick to call things movements. Why think we have already learned all there is to know about something that has been happening for centuries but that we are just starting to grasp?

A new global language for Christianity is being talked about, and we've barely scratched the surface. In the end, I think *we will have* a global church planting movement. I think it can and will happen. Why are the nations given eternal status in Revelation? Is there any other institution that has that kind of longevity in the Bible? I believe this is from the hand of God and a signal of things to come.

The New Math

$JM \times C + NT = CPM$

When a Jesus movement (JM) exists, it multiplies while simultaneously multiplying the church (C). When you then add the possibility of a new territory (NT) or a new nation to the mix, then and only then do you get a church planting movement (CPM).

Chapter 3

MULTIPLICATION IS LOCAL CHURCH DRIVEN

LCD x 10% = M

I'll never forget the first time I met Brian Bloye. We were speaking together at an event and wound up sharing a meal together afterward. Over dinner, he shared with me his dream of planting several churches out of his church. I could see everything he was describing happening in the near future because he was so determined. And it did happen. In my opinion, there is not a young megachurch pastor in America who emulates more what the church should look like than Brian Bloye. His story illustrates how one local church can multiply itself many times over.

> **Blog posted by Brian Bloye**
> Pastor, West Ridge Church, Dallas, GA
>
> When we first got involved in church planting, it was basically all about sending money. Early on we financially supported several church plants all over the country. Then we started sending groups of people to help these churches to do things like canvas neighborhoods, run a VBS, and help with launch services. All of this was great, but I felt God telling me that it wasn't enough. If God was going to build another megachurch in the South, it had to be about more than one church. I felt God telling me that West Ridge was put on this earth not just to support church plants but to help start them.

In 2003 we hired our first Church Plant (CP) intern. It was an amazing experience for our church. It really helped us get the focus outside of not only the walls of our church but also the confines of our community. Our focus was now stretching beyond the region that God had called us to reach ... we were now focusing on another region of Atlanta. It created a buzz in our church. We sent out eight families with our first intern. That church has grown to nearly 800 people.

What will fuel the coming global CPM? Local churches. Networks, denominations, and church planting organizations all have their place—that of servicing local churches. However, we must be absolutely clear about this: churches start churches. And they cannot pay someone else or another organization or even fund a network they are a part of to do what God has specifically called and empowered the local church to do—start churches.

The very best resources will come not from denominations or organizations but from practitioners in the field who are involved in movements. It all begins there. There should be standards, accountability, and processes that are uniform and organized. However, the irony is that no network, organization, or denomination will have a future in the global CPM unless the churches that are affiliated with it are in the fields. The failure of local churches to be deeply entrenched in church multiplication is the death knell of any hope of a global church planting movement.

Living the Parable of the Talents

Multiplication is living out the parable of the talents;[1] it's just a matter of the amount for which you want to trust God! If ever there was an application for the parable of the talents, it is for church planting. You remember the story of the man who entrusted his property to three servants and the results each one achieved.

At NorthWood, we initially planted churches; then they began to multiply. They multiplied not because we have a foolproof system. It had then and, frankly, continues today to have holes in it. But it worked because we built the concept of multiplication into the very fabric of what we taught our new churches to do. Like the servants in this story, the more we trusted God, the more he gave us.

If anyone understands multiplication, it's Bob Buford—not just church multiplication but the multiplication principle in general! I don't know anyone in the entire world like him—he's in a category all by himself. Bob doesn't have to be an expert on something; he just sees something cool happening and gets involved with it (or pours gas on it).

His motto is 100x—find something going well and multiply it 100 times. For years, he was a businessman. Having made his fortune, he invested it and used some of it for various ministry and humanitarian endeavors. I don't know everything he's involved in, but one venture he started is called Leadership Network—an organization for pastors of growing churches. His plan has been to gather the sharpest people in the room on a given subject and then turn them loose. He may or may not provide some funding, but most important he gets the right people in the room who are already doing church planting. He brings in consultants and people most pastors never have access to, and then lets us learn from one another and improve what we do.

One day Dave Travis and Linda Stanley, who both work for Leadership Network, asked to meet with me to discuss starting a new learning community for churches and organizations that were starting churches. At first, we planned one church every three years. Then we settled on one church a year, then inched it up to two a year. They asked me, "What would it take for you to start more churches a year?"

I said I'd have to think about it. (I came up with some astronomical financial amount—you only get one shot at this sort of thing. All they can do is say no, so you don't want to be chintzy!)

I think they gave me perhaps 25 percent of what I asked for—and off we went. We started learning from others, organizing, and developing our own system. At first, it was just our church. However, we grew to starting ten churches a year—and then we had granddaughter and great-granddaughter churches. Finally, we grew to a point where we formed a network for our churches and other churches that wanted to affiliate with us, called Glocalnet.[2]

Glocalnet—an Organic Church Network

Glocalnet has become NorthWood's organic network of churches that came out of her. One year seventy-five churches were planted from that little network! However, a huge lesson I had to learn was that most of those churches came from only about 25 percent of the churches we had started. Many wanted to be a part of a network that would do something like that, but the majority of them didn't have skin in the game.

We've never had a get-together of just "us," but we are about to and I'm really excited about that. Recently, we lost the person who was over our church planters. Instead of replacing that person, the NorthWood staff and I began to do the training ourselves. What was meant to be a stopgap measure has become our standard practice. It's how we are going to do it not just in the interim but in the future. The response of the interns was that instead of working with someone who had come from outside—as good as that person may be—they wanted to be with someone who had made NorthWood what it was. When the network became an organization, my role had to change. I look forward to recapturing some of what it had been in terms of the relationships.

How did all this happen? We just grabbed what was in front of our face each time something came from God, and the result has been awesome. Recently, I've been dreaming about what it would look like for a single local church to plant a hundred churches a year. With each church at the end of its first year around a hundred members, that would put the total number of members somewhere around ten thousand a year! Sound crazy? I never would have thought we would be planting ten churches a year! So why not a thousand per year? Hey, what about a hundred thousand per year?

Multiplication Works for Networks

Something else unexpected was happening. As different planters in various cities began their own churches and began to plant others, their focus narrowed on their own city network of planters. It became harder to relate to a national network—which was a good thing. Ultimately, these new planters wound up with their own local networks! Our network was unintentionally helping to spawn other networks. That angle of multiplication had never crossed my mind.

One of the key lessons I've since learned is that multiplication works for churches as well as networks. The order is important; hopefully the local network emerges not as an end in itself but out of necessity because the work is already being done. It is a positive move when a network multiplies because it leads to more effective strategic collaboration. If you try to hold it too tightly and organize it, you just may wind up with something you don't want—a cumbersome institution!

Today, everyone is starting networks. However, only those that form as a result of function (not because they want a network) will survive. In other words, local churches must be the ones planting the churches, not the organization or the network.

I have had the opportunity to get to know Al Weiss, the president of Disney Theme Parks Worldwide, and Steve Johnson by serving on the board of their organization called Vision360. Vision360 exists to plant churches through societal engagement that leads to community transformation glocally. I met them at a time when Al, the chairman of the board, and Steve, the president of Vision360, were in the process of putting the organization together. At the time, Glocalnet was growing and I had to do something to manage it. They asked me to be a part of their new group along with other people. I knew at the time that it could be either an awesome blessing or a curse.

Here's why. I challenged them to not start another church planting organization, but to be the hub of a collaborative group of churches that were already doing this across the country. If they did that, I'd want to be a part.

In certain cities, someone's name will inevitably come forward in conversation as a potential contact for a church planter who wants to plant in that city. It's usually a senior pastor who planted his church in that city and is now planting other churches. Realizing the key to multiplication is churches planting churches, we invited just a handful of pastors who would want to spend a couple of years getting all the systems in place. After we worked the kinks out of the systems, we would then go into more cities, serving as a hub to bring all the various networks together. We would both provide services and plant churches.

Five churches turned into ten, and then ten to fifteen, and now close to twenty are a part of Vision360, representing that many cities. We aren't starting a new organization; we're merely linking arms, raising money together, and refusing to be turf-oriented (see Figure 8). We aim to agree on basic standards and practices together to get the job done. What is also incredibly exciting to me is that the key players driving this idea are businesspeople and nonclergy. I love that because for the most part religious organizations and professionals have driven church planting.

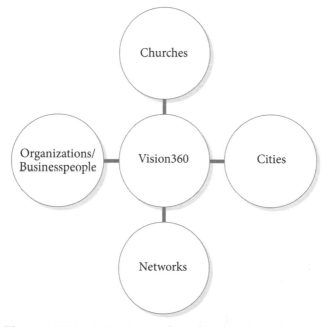

Figure 8: Vision360 exists to plant churches through societal engagement that leads to community transformation glocally.

The Tithe of the Local Church

Multiplication is the tithe of the local church. By that I mean it's just simple obedience. God has called churches to multiply. Living things reproduce; dead things don't! Most pastors would freak out if their core leadership didn't tithe, witness, or serve. How do you think God looks at churches that don't multiply? No big deal? Think again.

Here is a simple question: If a church could reach a hundred people, but instead reached only ten lost people, would it be disobedient not to reach those other ninety? Generally speaking it would. What if a church could reach a thousand instead of a hundred, or ten thousand instead of a thousand? You get the picture.

How Do You Do It?

At this point, people's questions mainly have to do with "how." How do we start all these churches with church planters and core groups? Studies have shown that a church can hive one time. Some can do it twice. Rare is the church that can do it three times. Hiving is intentionally sectioning off a part of your church to go and start another one (see Figure 9). No matter what size the original mother church, it takes five years to regain the leadership group lost during the hiving process. That makes sense because the top percent of entrepreneurial people in the church will want to start the new church.

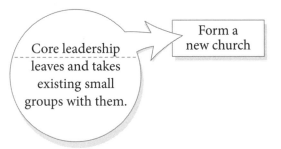

Figure 9: Hiving
Hiving is skimming off the top percentage of leadership to
start a new church; it takes five years to regain.

Instead of stretching to be the rare church that can hive three times and start three churches, we use a different system. We look for church planters to start a core group from scratch, not planters who have to have a ready-made church handed to them (see Figure 10). If we planted churches primarily through hiving, we could not continue to plant the number of churches we plant, nor could we do it at the rate that we plant them. We would be constantly skimming off our leadership.

That said, I'm not against hiving. Often we'll have families in NorthWood who choose to go with one of our church planters to start a new church. That's natural, common, and normal. However, we do not have a "calling out" service fifteen times a year to start fifteen churches.

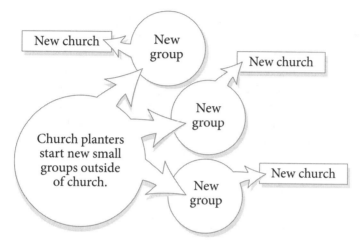

Figure 10: Forming New Core Groups
Church planters begin new core groups from people outside the
church that seed several new church-starting churches.
The process repeats itself in every new church.

Awhile back, I was with a "giga-church" pastor whom I greatly respect and believe in. I told him, "Look at what we're doing with just two thousand. Think, man, what you could do with 15,000!" We need new metrics! If that church invested just one million dollars a year, using our simple system, it could plant as many as seventy churches in a year! At a minimum of one hundred in attendance at the end of the first year, that would translate into a total of seven thousand a year!

If they had done that for ten years and things were proportionate to a specific size and number, that church could have seen one million people follow Christ and become a part of one of those churches! All of a sudden, 15,000 looks like a scrawny cow ready to be turned out to pasture. I know God does the saving, and I understand these are just metrics—but what metrics! I'd love to stand before God having been a part of something that yielded a million people over a ten-year period! I really want it to be a billion—why not dream big? How about seven billion—the world population today?

The key is to think "movement"—and act "multiplication." There can be no doubt that movement is the work of the Holy Spirit. However, multiplication is the simple obedience of local churches. There may be nothing any of us can do about starting a movement, but there is a lot we can do about multiplication! We wouldn't want a person leading our church who didn't tithe, so why would we want pastors leading large churches that don't multiply?

What Multiplication Looks Like

Multiplication is what local churches must continue to do throughout their life cycle to ensure that the gospel goes forward in their country. As I have explained, there is no historical evidence that after the gospel first invades a country, it does so a second time. The initial movement of the gospel is powerful in a specific place. Whereas the initial movement travels across the culture of secular domains (education, business, medicine, etc.), the subsequent ones travel across established religious networks. The only hope for the growth of faith at that point is multiplication. Although not as fast as movements, multiplication nonetheless becomes the fuel that grows the church for future generations.

It isn't that this phase is less important—just different. At this point, resources are acquired and it becomes a "sending" church that has the resources to invest in other nations. What has become institutionalized now provides the base for something else, something new, to go viral.

Multiplication is what a kingdom church looks like. Where the kingdom is, it always spreads. It's the mustard seed; once the seed is planted and takes root, it takes over and is all-encompassing. Jesus said, "The kingdom of heaven is like a mustard seed, which a man took and planted in his field. Though it is the smallest of all your seeds, yet when it grows, it is the largest of garden plants and becomes a tree, so that the birds of the air come and perch in its branches" (Matthew 13:31–32).

It is possible to have a church without the kingdom. However, you won't have the kingdom without multiplying churches. Church multiplication matters like nothing else and is the "Acts" plan of expanding the kingdom in communities where the gospel constantly moves forward.

Multiplication is the hope of the future and the potential base from which the church will expand globally. Without multiplication, the movement cannot be sustained and the institution will die. The early days of most institutions are focused on how you establish the standards and propel your movement further. Another positive aspect of institutions is that when they emerge, they serve as the financial and organizational base for churches to do large-scale things that they can't do alone.

I know that some would passionately disagree with the concept of the institution having any positive aspects. As I mentioned earlier, I did as well for years. However, having worked in development in different nations and having seen the church develop, I've come to realize that, good or bad, institutions hold the historic values of people who brought us something we desperately need. Where institutions go wrong is when they make sacrosanct the methods, practices, and processes as opposed to the ideas. When this happens wholesale, that institution will ultimately turn on itself and die.

At best, institutions are the remains of our stories and embody the values necessary to engage the world. At worst, they confuse methodology with value. Regardless, there is no sustainability or future without the multiplication of churches. The highest demonstration of maturity for a local church is when it multiplies. Only something alive can reproduce, and it will do so only if it is healthy.

A Member of Two Churches, If That's What It Takes

If all this is so important, then why don't churches multiply?

Ignorance. Some people have never been a part of a new church. They grew up in an established church that had been there for years, or when they did begin going to church, the church they attended was older and had never planted before. This is also true of some pastors. Although they may know a church planter and be somewhat familiar with church planting, it isn't something they have ever been a part of.

I believe every Christian should be a part of at least one new church plant. Yes—even pastors! It doesn't mean they have to pastor the church, but they can be a part of it. I'd go so far as to say you could be a member of two churches, if that's what it takes. There are some things present in a new church that are just not present anywhere else. If you experience it, it will pervade every way you do church.

Church leaders are awakening to the idea that multiplication can happen at any point in their ministry. A pastor in his fifties recently came up to me at a conference to tell me about how God had given him a vision for his church to start a new church. They did so, and awhile later they planted another one. The pastor recalled watching with envy the enthusiasm of the new pastors in these new churches and the growing excitement until he just couldn't stand it anymore! "It nearly drove me crazy," he said, because he wanted to be a part of something new like that. So, at the age of fifty-one, he resigned his church and is now in the process of planting a new church where the church-planting DNA is imparted deep inside.

Distraction. Some models of discipleship actually get in the way of multiplication. Pastors or leaders may feel they have to get their own converts on their feet first before they can start another church. Once they get the whole church healthy and strong, they will get around to planting other churches. This model does not stand the test of Acts. Discipleship isn't information transfer but behavioral transformation, which is one of the principles I am most passionate about.[3] The way we approach discipleship is a huge factor in whether or not we multiply other churches. What if being a good disciple meant being a part of a new church?

Delay. Some pastors believe they cannot start a church until they first grow their church to a large size and make them debt-free. Some will say they are waiting until their church gets "healthy"—and that is defined so many different ways. Those who say, "We aren't big enough yet," especially when they have a hundred people, don't have an accurate definition of church.

Competition. Let's just be honest about it—some people don't start churches because they are afraid of the impact it may have on their own church. I am a pastor, and I am talking about pastors! People without Jesus couldn't care less if you start a church. However, Christians and even members of existing churches actually become proud of their churches for starting new churches. Early on, I learned that the biggest obstacle to planting other churches is other pastors. Even the devil is no match for them! Holy ambition and competition are the highest forms of spiritual pride. Arrogance enslaves us to the point of Pharisaism.

Laziness. Starting a new church takes work—and some churches don't want to work. They want to do their own thing and don't want to have to be responsible for anyone outside their own four walls.

Lack of oxygen. Any church that doesn't or won't multiply is just plain dead!

Benefits for Every Church

Every church that multiplies extends its own life cycle.

Every church has a life cycle—and that isn't bad, contrary to what some people think. The fact that some local churches eventually die is not always negative; it can actually be a positive thing. The question is, Are you planting more churches than are dying because of a shifting population, a new focus, and other factors? Starting churches roots you firmly in the future; you're a part of what God is going to do in a future generation. As a church becomes more effective at church planting, it is able to plant churches in other cities, states, and even nations. The result is the extension of a local church far beyond its own boundaries.

One huge benefit of church planting at NorthWood is how it has kept us relevant and near what God is doing. Nothing has kept us on the edge like church multiplication. Models and methods come and go from one generation to the next. The older a church or pastor gets, the more entrenched they can become in their own particular model of church, whether seeker, innovative, contemporary, postmodern, house, and so on. Because there is always a forward thrust to the faith when you are helping young people start churches, it has an impact on your own local church.

Every church that multiplies passes on a story—not methods.

All of us are part of a greater story. As we began to plant other churches, I became curious about the story of NorthWood. I wound up doing a family tree of our church and found an amazing history of church planting. Our church was sponsored in 1985 by North Richland Hills Baptist Church. However, nearly thirty years earlier, in 1956, NRHBC was sponsored by Richland Hills Baptist Church, which was also the result of church planting. RHBC was sponsored in 1953 by Birdville Baptist Church. And Birdville was sponsored in 1856 by a small church named Lonesome Dove Church, which just happened to serve as author Larry McMurty's inspiration for the name of a Western series, *Lonesome Dove*. It was the first Protestant church west of the Mississippi, founded by John Freeman and a handful of families who moved to Northeast Tarrant County in 1849.

I went looking for Freeman's grave at that church one day. I found the graves of some of his relatives, but not his. Knowing what I do about his fervor for church planting, I shouldn't have been surprised. Along with a friend, Noah T. Byars, the two of them planted churches up and down the state of Texas. Then he left in 1854 to start one of the first Protestant churches in Southern California because of the gold rush, planting churches all along the way. He lived until 1918 and died sharp as a tack at the age of ninety-eight! Is there any wonder why NorthWood plants churches? That man passed something on down through his story!

This lesson in NorthWood's history demonstrates the biggest benefit of all. Church multiplication allows a church to pass on its DNA. For us, to be able to pass on core principles such as the idea of the kingdom, "glocalization," transformation, discipleship based on behavior versus information, and design all matter. If we pass down those transferable qualities, then any church can always be relevant.

Every church that multiplies more than one church a year generally sees the expression of multiple models of church planting.

The goal is to reach the community (as opposed to extending a single model). I love every kind of church. My goal is never to promote a single model. I tell our interns that if they leave NorthWood and plant a church just like NorthWood, they've failed. Each church must be unique, designed according to its own culture and context. I want to pass on values and narrative, not methods.

> **Blog posted by Bob Roberts Jr.**
> **January 26**
>
> On more than one occasion, I've found myself in a group of mega-church pastors who make a statement like this: "We need to partner to start some significant churches — we don't need to waste our time on these little churches of a hundred or two hundred. We want to start a thriving, large church." They don't get it! I try to educate them, but, more often than not, to no avail. When they make a statement like that, they miss two things. First, they don't know their history. Where faith has exploded, it has never been because of the multiplication of mega-churches, but of smaller churches from 50 to 200. This happened in the early church, Europe and throughout American history, and now it is happening in Asia. Nothing wrong with a mega-church, if that's what God has for a church. NorthWood is a mega-church, BUT to not know history is to make some major mistakes. Second, they don't understand the nature of movements. Movements are personal and viral. Where movements have emerged, it hasn't been because of the large, but because of the small. There is a difference between a fad and a movement. A fad is short-lived.

Every church that multiplies, once it starts, finds that only time and apathy will slow it down.

Once a church starts multiplying, it keeps on multiplying. This is why the new plants out of NorthWood are expected to help plant a church within their first year. Is it because running one to two hundred a month is going to make or break another new church? I don't think so. What we are doing is setting the DNA or determining the stem cells. Doing so is more for the benefit of the one-year-old church than for the brand-new church. The church planter who has been out there for one year can meet at least once a month with the brand-new planter if for nothing else than to just encourage him. Most planters need encouragement more than new ideas! They're filled with new ideas.

Every church that multiplies is really a big church.

By that I mean it sees the church as bigger than the Sunday event. The church is bigger than its attendance and greater than its building. To multiplying churches, the church is huge. They value the whole body, not just a building and one local congregation. Churches that see only their own agenda and refuse to live in the broader context of the universal church will never be a part of the coming global church planting movement.

When a church is physically and literally large, the leaders need to ask the question, "Why did God make us so large?" They need to ponder why he gave them the resources he did and what he expects as a result. I used to be under the impression that if we started a lot of churches, we would always be small—kind of like pruning ourselves back each year. That wasn't the case. We wound up growing.

However, there is no guarantee that by multiplying churches you will grow large. There are times when multiplying churches has interfered with our resources at home and what we could do there. However, the bigger picture must always win. Those of us who pastor large churches, though our model may not be as reproducible, possess a "nursery" or incubator with the capacity to be much larger than most churches, and we should use it as much as possible. I believe God gives us resources not just for ourselves but for others.

Every church that multiplies measures outside its walls.

Churches that multiply don't measure everything inside their four walls. They measure their plants. They measure the young people who leave who are doing ministry vocationally and in their own specific professions. I didn't initially anticipate how many of our young people would wind up going into the ministry because they had seen us starting other churches and working globally. There is no doubt in my mind that if we did not do the things we do, we would not have that many going into the ministry. Most people have defined the ministry only in terms of what they see the church doing, and usually that means what the church does on Sunday. At NorthWood, they see something else.

A couple of years ago, I began to see some of the interns who had grown up as children at NorthWood learning to plant everything from house churches to third space churches. Our relationship is far beyond models, however. It's organic and those interns know that I'll always be there for them. They're not some "way out" or "weird" church planters or community developers. I consider them family and I know that they are there for me as well. The primary relational focus in church multiplication is the church and the disciple—not the pastor and the denomination, network, or organization. This is precisely what we are missing in the West, but it must be recovered if we ever get to church multiplication status as a whole.

Creating a Climate for Church Multiplication

If you want to create a climate conducive to church multiplication, make sure that the church planters you are going to send out are a part of your church and your people see them and know them. Our internship program keeps church planting in front of our people. They meet all the young pastors on their first Sunday with us. We bring them up as a group in all the services and give them an old skeleton key to remind them that they are here to learn about the kingdom of God. We instruct them that they are to be a part of the kingdom and extend it as far as possible. We then have people lay hands on them and we pray for them as a group.

The church planting interns start small groups in our church, so they are part of our normal, ongoing community. They get to "take with them" anyone they reach in their small group, keeping in mind that the majority of their people are going to come from outside NorthWood. If they can't start a small group, why should they think they can start a church? If all they do is gather existing church members for their small group, they haven't indicated their ability to plant a church. When they gather people from outside NorthWood, we start getting excited.

When the planters leave at the end of their internship, we have a special service for them. I call on a child or teenager from the service to tell the group the legend of St. Christopher (as best they can!). The legend that they are all familiar with goes like this: Late in the day, a little boy persistently asked an old man to help him cross the river. Even though the old man had just crossed from the other side, the boy pleaded with him to return so that he could get home to his parents. The old man finally agreed to help him cross back over, although he was very tired from having just crossed himself.

Halfway there, he was exhausted and told the child, "I feel like I'm carrying the weight of the world when I carry you!"

When the old man eventually made his way to the other side, the little boy reached up and hugged the old man around the neck and said, "Thank you, Christopher—you are a saint!"

Smiling, the old man reciprocated the hug and replied, "Now hurry home, Jesus. Joseph and Mary are waiting."

The name Christopher means "Christ bearer or carrier"—which to me is a reminder to them that these church planters have been called to carry the good news of Jesus around the world in a similar fashion.

I then go down the line and each planter tells the congregation where they will plant their church in the United States and which difficult country they will work in globally. We then lay hands on them and pray for them as a group. It's impossible to minimize the profound impact this ceremony has on a child growing up at NorthWood. They see it twice a year, every year, and it leaves a powerful impression.

Whenever church planters are back in town, I like to interview them briefly and pray for them. At other times, others we are working with across the country or around the world visit our church. If I know it ahead of time, we always recognize them and pray for them. What you do publicly is what you value and what you endorse, and that contributes to the overall culture you are trying to create.

Continually planting churches around you demonstrates your commitment to churching your area. A young man came over to my wife when she was in Starbucks recently and thanked her for the time she lets me spend with him as he is planting his church. My son has been attending that new church some. It has around a hundred people—but in our culture, that church has as much value as (and maybe requires more attention than) a church that is huge! This pastor simply overheard her talking about NorthWood and our upcoming trip to Vietnam. Some other members were present with her at the time. It was an invaluable moment as they all got to spontaneously see the impact their church is having on other churches.

The New Math

LCD x 10% = M

Local Church Driven (LCD) is the key to sustainable multiplication. Ten percent (10%) of the membership is the tithe of every local church to plant churches. When that happens as naturally as any other ministry in the church, we will multiply (M) like never before.

Chapter 4

STARTING CHURCHES IS NOT ENOUGH

K (M/I/O/C/G/E) = T

"Why do we start churches?" If we fail to ask ourselves this important question — or fail to answer it — we will wind up doing something for no reason at all (which is par for the course both in education and in religious work!). Starting a church for the sake of starting a church is not a good reason. Starting a church because God has brought hungry, seeking people into your circle of influence is a good place to start, as the following story from one of our interns, Aaron Snow, demonstrates.

On a personal level, the most exciting part about starting churches is to see young people come up through the ranks of NorthWood, find Christ, and then begin planting their own churches as young adults. Aaron has been a part of NorthWood since he was four years old. I have vivid memories of chasing this high-energy kid around Children's Camp, threatening to send him home if he didn't settle down. I remember having to pull him off bigger, stronger kids when he lost his temper just before they killed him. Today, Aaron has earrings, tattoos, and hair in every conceivable place, but God's hand is all over this young man and I love him deeply.

> Blog posted by Aaron Snow
> NorthWood intern graduate/church planter, Las Vegas
>
> About seven months ago, the Lord began breaking our hearts for the unchurched — those who had been "burned" by a church "gone wild," or who had never stepped foot into a church building for whatever reason. We began thinking that *someone* has

to reach out to these people! This could be a 20-year-old college kid, a homeless man, or a homosexual drug addict. (All of which have been along for this ride.) Either way, these people had one thing in common: the idea of walking into a church building on a Sunday morning made them laugh. For whatever reason, they had a very skewed view of Christ, what He was about, and what it meant to live a life radically and unashamedly in love with HIM. What would it look like if we, as the hands and feet of Christ, actually began LIVING out the Gospel with reckless passion!?

We began spending a lot of time at a local Starbucks meeting the most random people and building relationships with them. This led to weekly gatherings at Starbucks, IHOP, or whatever "third space" location made sense for that particular moment in time. Eventually, we made our way back to one of our condos. This is where "Intentional Gatherings," or "I.G.s" was birthed. It shifted from just hanging out "intentionally," to being a little more organized and planned. (Please know that without that first stage things would never have gotten where they are.) We began doing extensive work with the homeless in downtown Ft. Worth. What had happened right before our very eyes was something beautiful, something only God could have done. A "missional community" had developed; a group of people who loved the Lord with such a passion that it poured over into every second of their every day. Every moment was an opportunity to live out the gospel...

The interesting thing is that our goal with I.G.s was never to fill our living room full of people, or even be a part of a movement. We simply obeyed, and found ourselves in the middle of one. Please know that this ALL happened very naturally. It was unplanned and unexpected. We had no intentions of "planting anything," or even starting anything for that matter. We simply asked what it would look like if we, as friends, started intentionally living out the Gospel every second of every day. In the midst of this, our group grows. We are reaching the point of multiplication. This is our desire. This is the vision. Our desire is not to cram 50 people in our living room causing us to need a building. Our desire is to see hundreds of "missional communities" all over the DFW area, and thousands all over the country. There are already hundreds that we know of all over the world. I've been asked a lot lately, "Are missional communities considered local churches? Are they legit?" You bet. We have been called, as the body of Christ, to BE the Church, not just GO to church.

I have heard some compelling reasons for starting churches over the years—but in and of themselves they are not enough. A church can start for a variety of such reasons, yet still not make a difference in people's daily walk with God and not even come close to making a difference in their community and the world at large. In the past ten years, church planting has gone from being the ministry position of last resort to the position of first preference.

I recently spoke at a conference in Orlando, Florida, where 1,800 pastors showed up, many of them young men, to learn about church multiplication. The ground is obviously shifting. That's good. However, if these new churches fail to go beyond merely being a Sunday event, then each will fail dramatically. Until we are planting churches that are dramatically changing our communities, cities, and nations, we will not achieve what God has called us to do.

One of the most exciting young church planters I know is Kevin Colon, who planted a church out of NorthWood four years ago in one of the most difficult places for church planters on earth—Superior, Colorado. In his tenure there, five churches came in and tried to get started, but none survived. From day one, he understood that the only way Cool River Community Church would fare better was by engaging the community and working around the world to make a difference.

His plan succeeded. Last week, I received an email from him saying he now has three other pastors—two in house churches and another pastor like himself—who want to plant churches all over Denver as a group. Cool River is a church under two hundred people, but they're ready to start planting all over the city! Knowing the difficulty of this undertaking, I suggested that he look to two or three other larger churches to get their support. His response floored me. "No, Bob. If [church planting] is not in their DNA, they can have all the money in the world, but it will never work."

Now that church planting is becoming the first choice of new ministers, we have to be careful that it doesn't appeal to us on the basis of what is "successful" and tied to our own ego. We can set ourselves up not to be salt and light in a community but instead superstars and icons. That may work for politicians, entertainers, and others, but for those who have been called to be salt and light—motive is everything. God wants us to succeed—but at his work, not ours.

Are These Reasons to Start a Church?

Let's look at a few of the top reasons people often point to when wanting to start a church.

The Great Commission. As Christians, we believe that we have a responsibility to fulfill what Christ has called us to do. The most obvious way to fulfill the Great Commission is to share the good news of Jesus Christ. This is what churches do. But this is not enough—many have gone out in the name of the Great Commission and left things worse than before they had come! Matthew 28:18–20 says, "Then Jesus came to them and said, 'All authority in heaven and on earth has been given to me. Therefore go and make disciples of all nations, baptizing them in the name of the Father and of the Son and of the Holy Spirit, and teaching them to obey everything I have commanded you. And surely I am with you always, to the very end of the age.'"

Evangelism. Church planting has been called the greatest method of evangelism ever created. There is no doubt about it—according to many different research sources, new churches reach the lost better than anyone or anything else. But even this is not enough; just getting people to pray the prayer and jump in the water alone doesn't change things.

Relevance. Because most new churches are planted by younger pastors and leaders, they tend to be more relevant in terms of communication. As the gospel is carried forward—generation after generation—each church planter must take the seed of the gospel and plant it in their context. Charles Kraft once said that the seed of the gospel will grow in any plant. And that is true—the gospel was made for any plant. But this is not enough; relevance can lead to a super consumerism that undermines the church.

Research and development (R&D). If all your church plants are succeeding, then chances are you're playing it too safe. Church planting gives us an opportunity to try things that established churches might not be able to get away with. Even if an experimental form of church planting doesn't work, you still haven't lost. Think about the lessons you have learned and what might be done by other churches. Churches like Willow Creek, Saddleback, Mars Hill, Solomon's Porch, and others can do things that the rest of us can learn from and implement. But this is not reason enough to start a church. The church is more than a test tube baby with which we can experiment.

Base heads. One of the exciting things about starting churches is that some are going to serve as base heads for their cities to reach others. Mars Hill Church, planted by Mark Driscoll in Seattle, has become a focus for reaching postmoderns and secular unchurched people by becoming a base head for planting churches. Some new churches emerging today will become teaching centers and church planting centers. Dave Ferguson at Community Christian Church in Naperville, Illinois, has become a teaching church for multisite churches and church planting. The list goes on and on. But this is not enough; the church can become someone's control center and yet, in reality, not be the bride of Christ.

Future generations. Churches planted twenty-five, fifty, or a hundred years ago will not necessarily be the ones to continue to reach future generations.

Church history has borne this out. They can, if the church is willing to reinvent itself, but sadly (or perhaps providentially) most do not. When the fondest thing you remember about a church is that "my great-great-grandfather helped start that church," you're in trouble. That's a good memory—as long as it isn't the first and most important memory. Each generation must plant churches in order to reach its own generation. But this is not enough; the church can be so niched that it has no real power.

Existing churches. The impact new churches have on existing churches is profound. I remember when only a few churches were known as "contemporary" or "innovative" in their approach. As time progressed, many of the established traditional churches offered a contemporary service, then ultimately adopted a "blended" approach. What church wants to call itself a traditional church anymore? New churches impact existing churches in time if they stay focused. But this is not enough. Churches today teem with turf wars and competition; appealing to humanity's baser instincts to grow the church will ultimately pollute us if not held in check.

Transformation. This is the only reason worth starting a church. If this is your reason, you'll get the other seven reasons—but you will also get so much more. When I first started our church, I challenged myself to dream as big as I could, and when it was so big that I couldn't wrap my dream around it, then I knew that God was in it because only he could do that! The only unfortunate thing in terms of my dream (and, I fear, the dreams of other young guys as well) was that I defined "big" in terms of attendance.

What if instead of dreaming about hosting 20,000 people in one Sunday worship service, I had dreamed of 1,000,000 people in worship in the first ten years because we had started a church planting movement out of our local church? How would that have shaped and changed our ministry?

What if instead of dreaming of a 7,000-seat worship center, I dreamed of clinics, schools, and community centers in the inner city? What if instead of envisioning a 150-acre campus, I saw orphanages around the world and microenterprises? What if instead of longing for about 100 full-time ministerial staff, we had 1,000 staff located all over the world? What if instead of wishing for half the community to attend our local church, the community threw parties to thank our church for all the things it was doing in the community?

There is absolutely nothing wrong with dreaming any of those things. But the question is, Where do you start in your dreaming—the church or the world outside the church? That determines everything. It determines how you organize, where you engage, and how you prioritize. The reality is that we've been starting with the "church" stuff and have done very little to engage the community and society as we always say we plan to do. What if someone started with transformation first?

Not without a Price

It's time for us to start churches that are making a difference, and I think some pastors are beginning to recognize this. Church people are saying loudly that this is what they want and that this is where we will get credibility from unbelievers. However, they often do not realize the impact it will have on them, their view of ministry and the church, and the sacrifices it will require. In the past, when the church engaged society, persecution was generally a part of the equation — or, at the least, a deeper level of service and ministry!

The plagues did more to grow the church, as believers served the sick and suffering (though they themselves were dying), than all the church meetings combined. Persecution matters because it calls the church to sacrifice and suffer. Today in the West, we can't force persecution, nor would we wish that upon anyone. However, practicing a life of ministry that requires sacrifice in every dimension of our lives can have the same effect on the church. We've seen it happen at NorthWood, and we know this is what drove the early church the first few years of her life before the persecution of Stephen.

In Acts 2:42 – 47, believers were meeting, praying, worshiping, and selling their possessions and giving them away. When was the last time you saw a revival that led to people giving away everything they had? What impact would it have on us to believe in Jesus so much that we literally gave away our possessions? The church was birthed out of incredible ministry and service to one another. Yes, persecution did come, but something preceded the persecution — great personal sacrifice.

What Is a Transformational Church?
Not a False Impression: A Kingdom Church

My view of the kingdom of God has come so far. I used to believe that if only I could get people converted and into a church, we would change society. I was wrong. Until we see the kingdom of God as the plan of God in its entirety, we will never impact society. If transformation is taking place — personally, in the family, in the church, in the community, and in the nation — it's a sure sign that the kingdom is present. A kingdom church encompasses every sphere, sector, and domain of public and private life.

Jesus spoke often on the kingdom. We see the kingdom church emerging in Acts to change the face of the whole world. Throughout church history, the kingdom church brought hope. Christ is glorified and magnified in a kingdom church. It will be kingdom churches that bring radical transformation and will fulfill the Great Commission. Kingdom churches are holistic, comprehensive, self-sacrificing, and of necessity decentralized.

I am in Hanoi, Vietnam, as I write this. Some of the greatest impressionist painters of the world live and paint here. When the Communists came to power in 1954, the expression of art slowed down for a while. Yet the imprint of Van Gogh, Monet, and others remained deep on the Vietnamese from the influence of the French colonialists. Now, some of the greatest works of impressionism are found here, as well as some of the greatest "fakes" or copies! The artists line up their workstations on one particular street in Hanoi to do the painting. A painting that would ordinarily cost thousands is only fifty to seventy-five dollars, and the untrained eye would never be able to tell the difference between the original and a copy. I believe the church is like that today. Many impressions exist, but only God sees what the real one is really like.

What some of today's leaders are calling missional is what I would define as "kingdom." Missional simply means the kingdom flowing out of us wherever we are. It's living beyond ourselves and beyond what we can control. It's serving unexpectedly in places and spheres we never imagined. It's not relying on ourselves to do a human strategy that we can accomplish in our own strength. It's driven by a God who opens doors that we never could open.

> **Blog posted by Bob Roberts Jr.**
> **June 2**
>
> Everybody is talking "missional," but I don't believe they know what they mean by it. It has lost its meaning from what David Bosch started. Bosch quoted Martin Mahler saying, "Missions is the mother of theology," one of the points in a book Mahler read entitled *Choosing a Future of US Missions*.[1] The point is that missions isn't something you do — it is an expression of who you are. Who you are is how you live the kingdom. I don't like the word *missional*, but I used to. When it first came around, it communicated "missions is who I am and who we are as a people." However, today it has been redefined. To call things *missional* may be good, but I doubt that Bosch would have called it such.
>
> *Missional* — to use that word makes us feel good and "special." However, to redefine the word, or water it down, makes us think the Great Commission stops with us and our "culture," which makes the gospel tribal, not global.
>
> A better word for *missional* today is *relevance*. Most people using this are saying we are living incarnationally in our community. A lost man does that. He lives in his community and it's part of him, so he does social service and practices good

citizenship because we are all into "community." As preachers, we've learned to preach in relevant ways to our culture. That is fantastic, but it's not missional. Many postmoderns would consider themselves missional. I wouldn't. They're relevant — just like Robert Schuller was to his generation, Rick Warren to his, and now postmoderns are to theirs.

Schuller did it with the use of television and media. Rick Warren is doing it with his Peace Plan. It's crucial for church leaders today to learn what these guys did in order to build an army. But the fact that many people hear someone communicate does not make it missional. What makes it missional is when the army is deployed.

Are you still reading? To live relevantly in your own culture is survival. It's smart. It's good business. It's good education. It's good health. It's just good living that makes sense. Nonrelevant religious people in their community are simply sectarian. The goal isn't to make them "missional." They first have to be relevant. No one will be missional who isn't relevant. How can you speak to another culture if you can't even speak to yours?

So what is "missional"? It's living incarnationally beyond your own culture to the end of the establishment of the Kingdom of God. Living in your own culture is a given. I don't think you are really missional unless you are four steps removed from your own culture. One step removed means someone of your race but of a different tribe or homogenous unit. Two steps removed — that's a different ethnic group in your nation. Three steps removed — that's a Western culture or nation, though different, that still has Western underpinnings. Four steps removed is being around the least, the farthest, and the most different — it is the other side of the world. This requires loving like God. Jesus came to the "sick" that were nothing like Him, but He made the connection. This requires the Holy Spirit, the modern missionary to the transformation of the believer and his conformity to God.

So what difference does this make? First, those who love the farthest are the most effective in loving all the others. Second, those who love the farthest love like God; they connect us to what He cares about most and they model how He wants us to love.

Identifying with the World: An Incarnational Church — Connecting with a Fallen, Hurting World

Incarnational means we live with others — speak their language, feel their pain, and share their joy as well. We totally identify with them as Jesus did when he came from heaven to be with us. There could be no greater picture of what it means to live incarnationally with people than that of Mother Teresa. In doing so, she affected not just Calcutta, but the whole world. Some of you will be like me and dream of impacting the entire world. But I've learned credibility comes not from our dreams and grandiose statements about what we are going to do, but from what we have done. Capital is given not to dreamers, but to doers.

Also, when we practice incarnational living, we are most at risk of either shortchanging the gospel and making it easy believism or denying the exclusivity of Jesus Christ. The danger is that we can appeal to the base instincts of people to give them what they want. And a lot of times, when they are called to service, they don't want to take that call. On a Sunday morning they just look at you as if you are talking to someone else because in their minds, they've fulfilled their obligation to God — they showed up on Sunday! Because we love people and care about them, we can have a tendency to change the message. We cannot.

I recently spoke in Doha, Qatar, to a group of world leaders, including the former prime minister of Sudan, on faith and government. I was able to share how we work globally in various communities. Later, a key seminary leader complimented me and our church on what we were doing. However, her next question was, "But you really don't believe Jesus is the only way to God — you couldn't and do all you do, could you?" I smiled and told her with all sincerity, "I'm sorry to disappoint you, but that's exactly what I believe. And that is exactly why we do what we do. I believe that it serves as motivation for me to be sure I've done all I can."

Less to Divide Us: An Organic Church

The church in Jerusalem was organic — and very inward focused. The church in Antioch was not organically tied to the church in Jerusalem; it emerged on its own (except for the two businessmen from Cyrene and Cyprus who wound up there, according to Acts 11:19 – 21, but their intent was not to plant a church out of Jerusalem). Being organic is not a guarantee of effectiveness, but church planting movements globally are organic and tend to have more impact than unrelated scattered churches. However, if we are part of the body of Christ, we are all related.

He is the Head, not your "apostle" or "bishop." That means that North-Wood is organically related to Tony Evans at Oak Cliff Bible Fellowship and

Awakening Chapels with Ed Waken because we are all part of the body of Christ. Each of us may have our own system of government or organization — but if Jesus isn't the head of our churches, we're all in trouble.

We should be careful as we distinguish our movements and focus that we don't do more to divide us than bring us together. Amid our own unique traits and mission, we must never forget our broader connection to the body of Christ. This is one reason why I refuse to dismiss the church from 312 until the Reformation in 1517. If I do that, I've dismissed Augustine, Francis, Aquinas, Patrick, Hus, Tyndale, and a host of others. We must never forget that God has never been without a witness and has worked in movements throughout history in every single era.

That God would give some centuries greater exposure, love, and opportunity makes no sense theologically or practically. Just as ethnocentrism identifies one's own culture as best, history seems to have the same effect. We believe that no one has "gotten it right" until us!

One lesson I've learned is that ignorance is marvelous. The more we learn of God, people, history, and other fields of knowledge, the more we see things differently. Easy answers don't fit, and faith becomes more important. The more you learn, your faith will either become stronger or weaker.

On-the-Spot Creativity: A Contextual or Designed Church

Though churches are all connected organically, each church has to design itself based on its local context. There was a time in history when it was enough just to follow a specific model, but that's no longer the case. We are going to have to learn to think and design on the spot.

I grew up in a small East Texas town where your extracurricular activities were limited to two choices: play in the band or play football. I played football, and so did my buddies. Many of us also worked as sack boys at the local grocery store during the week. I remember a job none of liked to do was to stock the women's hosiery rack. I remember all of us laughing one time when we were stocking the rack with a particular brand of hosiery called "Big Mamas." Their slogan read, "One size fits every mama." On the back of the package, the size chart ranged from "Skinny Mamas" to "Medium Mamas" to "Big Mamas." "One size fits all" may work for hosiery, but it is not going to work in church planting, because church planting is the most niche marketed of all religious expression. The gospel is consistent, not the style.

Should a church plant be designed after its mother church? No. We talk about passing DNA from the mother church to the daughter church, but that has to do with the missional essence. It's one thing to pass on DNA; it's another to pass on skin tone, bone structure, and other biological features that will be shaped more by the context and era in which the church is planted. Multiplication takes into account the fact that new things happen in time. New churches have an opportunity to be more relevant to the culture around them than the mother church and can instantly update.

In previous years, when site development took place in the world, it followed a certain sequence. First, people would build new roads, add utilities, and then install various service items such as electricity, telephone, and water systems. That's no longer the case. When new technology comes along, a country like Cambodia that has just installed its whole communication system can be more current than the United States. It doesn't have to go back and progress through the history of the phone as we have; it starts with the technology at this point. Starting churches provides an incredible opportunity to engage the culture in the moment without worrying about responding to the past.

No Normal Boundaries: A Glocal Church

Kingdom churches aren't confined by the normal boundaries of most churches. There has never been a greater time to connect with the world globally than today.[2]

> What people are just now writing about and recognizing has quietly and unrecognizably been taking place for the past thirty years and has led to a glocal kind of world. Nothing local is purely local and nothing global is purely global. It has all intersected and created an open world on the internet and to a large but lesser degree in travel. It has allowed the village crafts girl in North Vietnam to sell her doll on the internet to a child in Weatherford, Texas.[3]

> Glocalization creates a massive opportunity for the church. The world has changed and opened like never before. The tragedy of the moment for the church is that in the West she views herself as a single-interest entity: the production of religious people and institutions. The prevalent view by evangelical believers is that the kingdom of God is concerned only about the sinner's prayer and the person being baptized. Whether it's the "star" evangelist or "superstar" pastor focusing on the Sunday event, the kingdom will be established not by human power or entertainment, but by the realization of God's concern for the whole of society and humanity. John 3:16 is about God's loving not just the whole geographic earth but also the whole of society.

> Be it a stadium event or the four walls of a church for the Sunday worship service, the future is about the decentralization of the church to where it's every person in every domain of society in the

pew connecting with domains and people globally. That is a radically different church from what we have seen and it will have radically different results that will be frankly more healthy.

It's not about missions; it's about globalization. People have become global beings. The problem with the word global is that it says "way over there." That is incomplete. It's way over there and here at the same time. That is why it's *glocal*. Missions is a religious response. Humanitarianism is a societal response. But if we look at Jesus, we will plant a healthy, holistic faith that has the ability to lovingly, not forcefully, transform society.[4]

Always Something to Learn: An Evolving Church

Blog posted by Bob Roberts Jr.
June 1

NorthWood has never been a tight church with a model to which we strictly adhered. When I was in my twenties, I discovered Rick Warren and the not-so-developed ideas back then of the Purpose Driven Church. As a young guy, I grabbed on to them after wrestling with them. I implemented them and our church grew. However, it didn't totally fit me or our church ... I was learning you have to be yourself, not someone else.

I felt the coming surge from post-modern and emerging churches. Many of the elements of our church reflected that without me understanding or, for a long time, realizing what was happening. As I learned, read, and experimented, I could get in the flow of what was going on and continue to see our church develop.

Gradually I began to discover the impact of glocalization on society and how that has had a huge impact on our church. It has been the most redeeming factor of our church, and probably the number one issue to position our church and engage society.

It ultimately led to my understanding of domains and infrastructures and how societies are developed and what God expects of us.

I'm having so much fun as I've woven three movements together. But, I know there will be at least two other movements I will see emerge, but what they are, I haven't a clue, yet. They will emerge out of what I'm currently involved in and I'll have to be alert to detect them.

I was with Loren Cunningham when I put all this together. I asked him how he had impacted the world so much. Obviously, there's no one answer to that, but here's what he said. First, God spoke to him about mobilizing the youth to engage the emerging generation. Second, he began to work with nationals — probably before anyone else — mobilizing them as missionaries. Third, he realized that 60% of the missionaries in the world are women, so he unabashedly worked hard to see women raised up in the ministry. (He and Cho fed off one another on that.) Fourth, he said that as a man now 70 years old, he had discovered spheres, domains, and infrastructures like me. That is what he is moving to drive now. But he *discovered* it 30 years ago. It may be that his best idea is the one he's now doing at 70!!!!! Most people would have retired long ago and just become preachers reminiscing about the good 'ole days. Not him.

Realizing this, I thought of a young pastor that I believe will be a leader in the future. I tried to explain this to him: "I believe you're good for three movements, four if you stay really sharp. Don't sign up for any of them; don't brand your hide. Think of them as waves to surf, getting God's people where they need to be. Each wave is important but not an end in itself. The end is Jesus. The wave is the rise of a generation. The surfboard is the method of riding or communicating. Don't stay with any wave too long — use your momentum to catch the next one. If your life and ministry is defined by a wave, you go one distance. If it's defined by surfing, well, that's another story."

Identifying the Prime Numbers

Starting churches really isn't enough. At the heart of all we are talking about is *what kind* of church we want to produce and multiply today and in the coming global church movement. More often than not, we start one step too quick and begin a church. We start a church with a lot of enthusiasm but without a clear understanding of what we are doing and why. "For I can testify about them that they are zealous for God, but their zeal is not based on knowledge" (Romans 10:2).

We can't say what kind of church we want to plant without first defining the church. Once we have that in mind, our mission is clear. Next, we have to identify the players who will get us where we want to go. I call them the prime numbers, and the players progress from pastors to planters to people in the pew to society and the world at large.

The New Math

K (M/I/O/C/G/E) = T

It's not enough just to start another church. It matters what *kind* of church you start. Only kingdom churches are worth planting. A kingdom church (K) is missional (M), incarnational (I), organic (O), contextual (C), glocal (G), and evolving (E). When you plant that kind of church, there is transformation (T).

THE PRIME NUMBERS

Chapter 5

APOSTOLIC FATHERS

Bf x ge + BP = AF

I didn't like turning forty, and fifty excites me even less! I felt disappointed at forty. I felt by then I'd have a church of 20,000. (My wife told me I preach as good as or better than Hybels and Warren and she should know!) But it didn't happen.

I stuttered severely as a child (so much so that my mom was the only person who could understand me!), so I never anticipated being a Billy Graham. I'd heard of D. L. Moody and a special Sunday school teacher who took notice of him and reached him for Christ. When I accepted the call to the ministry, I prayed to be like that Sunday school teacher. I said, "Lord, just let me raise up others if you can't use me to preach." (Miraculously, he healed my stuttering within a few months of his call, and I haven't shut up since!) I didn't know or understand at that time what church planting was. However, God was preparing me even then to value investing my life in others so that they could move the ball forward.

You can be Mark Driscoll, Rob Bell, Rick Warren, Bill Hybels, or Neil Cole, or you can be the person who raises them up. What role do you most want to play? I used to want to be them—to get to see all this stuff happening up close—but that's because all I saw was what I could do.

As I grew older and began to help planters start their churches, I realized I could have greater impact raising up multiple leaders who would plant more churches than I could ever do alone. Not all of us are gifted or called to be Driscolls, Warrens, or Coles, but every single pastor can raise up other young men and women. As a matter of fact, one of the chief roles and responsibilities of every pastor is that of raising up leaders—not just for their church but for the broader church as well.

Which is greater, to plant a single church or to plant multiple churches out of your church? Every single pastor gets to play in this game, at this level. Most of us grieve over what we perceive as our lack of ability and opportunity, and it causes us to overlook what we could be doing right where we are if only we would do it.

Celebrating the New Heroes

One of my heroes is a pastor named Mark Harris, pastor of Oasis Church in Tucson, Arizona. Mark, a businessman who went into the ministry, was on a megachurch staff before planting his own church in Tucson. Fifteen years later, Mark's church runs around 150, twice the typical church size in America—not bad. But it doesn't stop there—Mark's church in Tucson has planted about eighteen churches, and now on a given weekend, close to four thousand people are in church every single Sunday! Only 135 churches in the United States have four thousand or more worshipers—way to go, Mark! He has accomplished what only 135 pastors have done, but in multiple locations through multiple pastors.

By contrast, Brian Bloye, from Dallas, Georgia, shows how a larger church can do it. He started his church eight years ago and now has a church of four thousand. Two years ago, he started a church planting school at his church and they have planted multiple churches since. Large churches can bring so much to the table in terms of scale, which is why many people erroneously think only large churches are "big enough" to multiply. However, this can't be a large church thing only, or we'll never get to movement status. We must build the systems and structures for the typical-sized churches in the United States to reproduce.

If we ever get to church planting movement status, it won't be because we have all 1,200+ megachurches (churches with over two thousand in Sunday attendance) starting churches, but because we have opened the doors for all 400,000 churches to plant churches (see Figure 11). Churches that plant churches must be able to do it at a size of seventy-five, or it will never happen.

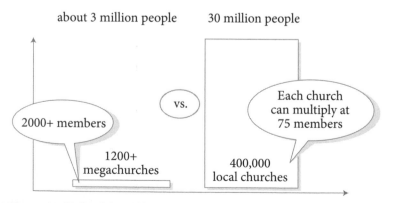

Figure 11: Unleashing All Churches to Plant Church-Starting Churches

The problem is that in American culture we value the megachurch pastor and superstardom so much that sadly, many megachurch pastors view those smaller churches as insignificant (please keep in mind I am a megachurch pastor). We must have a radical shift in how we value all churches and pastors in order to most effectively mobilize and deploy people to engage society.

David Phillips, pastor of Mission Fellowship Church in Middletown, Delaware, is a young pastor working on his doctorate degree. The church he pastors runs around fifty, but he has a goal to start multiple churches out of his church. He is in the process of starting his first church, but his goal is to start thirty churches in fifteen years. He wants them to be of every ethnicity and every kind. Pastors like him must become the new heroes if we really want to reach our nation.

So what is the message to those of us who are megachurch pastors? With our size and resources, I believe we have a larger responsibility to facilitate and help provide resources for new churches like no one else. As pastors (really bishops) of large communities, I believe that if we fail — or more likely simply refuse — to aggressively plant churches, God will hold us deeply accountable for using the church for our own end as opposed to extending his glory to the ends of the earth.

What Is an Apostolic Father?

Apostolic is a term that people use a lot lately. Not to be confused with the original twelve apostles, the word simply refers to one who is "sent." It's the picture of sending others out to engage the world. Today, what I call *apostolic fathers* is simply the sending part of the church. These are the people who are entrepreneurs and highly visionary; they believe anything is possible, especially when others don't. They are huge risk takers who not only see but begin moving toward that vision.

We need pastors who are apostolic — sending, leading by vision, enterprising, risk taking. An apostolic father is the kind of pastor who will wind up starting churches out of his church. What does that look like? You might be surprised at the first and foremost characteristic.

Broken

Pastors who raise up other pastors and plant churches out of their church are generally pastors who have been broken. This brokenness generally results from a failed attempt to achieve their own dreams as opposed to God's. In the ministry it is so easy to confuse our will with God's and to sanctify what we want to do by spiritualizing it or rationalizing it. The inevitable brokenness that results will drive a pastor either away from God or very close to him. If the pastor allows it to drive him close to God, invariably that pastor will discover the kingdom. I hear this same story played over and over again. Those who have been humbled and never want to go through that experience again often become gentle giants (something I'm still working on).

Missionary

Pastors who raise up other pastors and plant churches out of their church are generally "missionary" pastors. Pastors involved in church multiplication don't define church by their church or model or even philosophy of ministry. Instead, they approach it with a more holistic view of what God wants to do in a community. They approach their community first as missionaries seeking to church the area and second as pastors trying to establish a base for their work. This is opposed to first being a pastor of a specific church who hopes to get "big enough" and "strong enough" to start churches.

Giving

Pastors who raise up other pastors and plant churches out of their church are generally pastors who love to give away everything! It has been a long time since the church refused to hoard things — even in the ministry. By contrast, the leaders I'm describing will give away influence, relationships, and money — whatever the protégé needs. These leaders also wind up being discerning because there are so many people who would use a leader like this for their own ends. Often, this kind of leader must acknowledge the fact that people may use them and do the best they can not to become cynical.

Giving people are often naive people; it is tough on them emotionally when they find out all they were was a paycheck, a tool, or something someone wanted just for their own gain. We've all experienced it. Have you ever visited with someone when someone else more important walked in and immediately the person you were talking with moved on?

Leighton Ford once taught me a valuable lesson. When young men would meet with him, he noticed how often they had a list of things they wanted to talk about. However, some would rarely ask about him, his ministry, or his life. Another significant global business leader I know once told me that in spite of all he did on the behalf of others, few said thank you.

I don't think you can avoid these types of relationships or encounters — it's just life. But you can control how you respond to them. One thing I have learned is that we all have room for three close friends, twenty friends, and sixty people who know us pretty well. It is critical for you to learn as quickly as possible who's legit, who's real, who's with you, and whom you are with for the long haul, and then focus on those relationships.

See the Big Picture

Pastors who raise up other pastors and plant churches out of their church get the big picture and see something bigger than themselves. They recognize the fact that everything is working together and God will put the pieces in place. They live for the future and see all interruptions as God at work.

They are ready for whomever, whatever, whenever, and wherever. This blog entry from a trip to Vietnam with a delegation of pastors, governmental leaders, and Mark Galli from *Christianity Today* illustrates it better than I can explain it.

Blog posted by Bob Roberts Jr.
September 6

We went to Taphin and visited with the local People's Party Chairman and then a young Hmong House Church Pastor. I'd been there before, but when the pastors in our delegation saw it, they were as moved as I was the first time. He had his pews hewn out of wood and the pulpit leaning up against the walls. Tacked on all four sides of his house church were copies of the edict from the government on Resolution #1 passed last year for religious freedom. I felt as if I was in the presence of a godly man. Here are just a few questions and answers from a long interview:

Bob: Is there anything you need?

The Pastor: I would like more training. They have these denominations here, and I'm not even sure about the one I'm a part of. How are they different?

Bob: Young pastor, listen to me. I'm going to tell you something very important. You are our hero; you are closer to the Gospel than any of us. Keep doing what you're doing and don't worry about the denominations. We can't even keep them straight in America. It isn't your worry. Love God and serve Him just like you've been doing, and when we stand before God together, don't forget those of us at the back of the line.

Bob: What do you do to grow yourself in God?

The Pastor: I pray three times a day and we have services where we pray and teach. I try to read the Bible and follow it. I always seek God every day.

Bob: Do you understand the Bible?

The Pastor: Yes. It isn't that hard to understand. It's the story of how God loves us, how He wants us to live, and how He teaches us to live. I just try to follow it.

Bob: Do you have any questions about anything, doctrine, pragmatic questions, etc.?

The Pastor: No. I know that God loves us and God forgives us, and we should do the same and serve others.

Bob: How did you become a Christian?

The Pastor: I was troubled by evil spirits and I wanted to be free. I heard the good news of Jesus and He's the one who brought me peace from this. This is how people find God because they, too, are troubled by spirits.

Bob: Why did you become a pastor?

The Pastor: Because I heard God calling me.

Bob: Do you need anything?

The Pastor: A computer to keep up with my work and 100 Vietnamese and 100 Hmong Bibles.

Bob: OK guys, ante up, let's do it right now.

We drove him to Lao Chai and bought it. The ethos of the moment was just powerful. Vince Vo prayed in Vietnamese, Vince Antonucci in English, and the pastor in Hmong. We wept, we prayed, we encountered God — all of us — communists and all!

Mentoring Young Leaders

Only the pastors who are willing to mentor young leaders will be able to plant churches out of their church. Recently, in response to a blog I posted about our interns, I was asked about developing leaders. The following pointers are not meant to be complete but to represent some of what I'm reflecting on even now. I do not consider myself an expert in this area but a practitioner because of various ministries and projects in which I'm involved. From being a pastor, to discipling a group of men, to working with church planters, to being involved in global development projects, here is some of what I'm learning. What I teach and what I try to do are what people like Bobb Biehl, Bob Buford, Leighton Ford, Kent Humphreys, Chris Grant, Roy Fish, and more recently a prayer mentor named Vicky Porterfield have taught me. I learn more from our interns and others I work with than they probably get from me.

(1) Live the life and do the stuff you talk about. Bobb Biehl has taught me that credibility is gained by three threads: results, time, and character. Results are simply what is seen. People generally listen not because of what you know or what you did, but because of what you are currently doing. Character is who you are. No one is perfect and everyone has flaws. Time gives us the ability to see the good and bad and helps us filter counsel from someone. It is the ability to be consistent over time.

(2) Teach first from what you've experienced. Anyone can write or talk on a subject and yet not be a "doer." Those who "do" and those who "talk" often sound similar, at first. However, the deeper you go, the more you learn the differences. What may sound like semantics actually becomes a key issue. Those who "experience" it will generally read more and more because they want to understand more.

I've learned over the years that there are two ways to gain influence. One is by what you know — people want to hear you talk about that. The other is by what you do — people want to hear the stories of what you've done and how you did it. Teaching is passing on information. Mentoring is life-on-life. The more healthy experiences a mentor has, the more he or she has to share.

In the past five years, my life has become extremely busy and I've had to be more selective about my involvements. Speaking at conferences actually began to get in the way of some of the projects in which our church has been involved. I had to choose what really mattered. Did I want to be a speaker or a doer? I felt I was making sure to do the discipleship and mentoring. However, a few months ago, God spoke to my heart that I needed to be more engaged in those things, and I have.

I've had to say no to some other things that might seem important, but as Earl Creps recently wrote in *Off-Road Disciplines*, there is a discipline to passing the baton. It hasn't been a well-practiced discipline. We often fear letting go of things because of someone who may do it as good as us. But as John Maxwell has said, if someone can do it 80 percent as good as you, let go. When we don't let things go, we not only deprive others of getting in the game, but we also lose our own effectiveness.

(3) Let others be around you in your context. This is something I have to relearn repeatedly. Whether we are in church or overseas, or involved in a project or ministry, being together is crucial. People who are busy doing don't always have a manual or journal near them to write down everything while they are working. (And if they did, they wouldn't stop and write in it anyway.) They're caught up in what they are doing, and living it is their passion. So, it's important to allow people to watch you while you do it.

I've always wanted more education in international relations. In fact, I've considered getting a degree in it. A few months ago, I was at a meeting in D.C.

alongside a prominent professor from Georgetown. At a break, I began talking to him about getting a graduate degree to learn more and gain some credibility in a field. He stopped me and said, "You're living it. You're practicing what those guys I teach come to school to learn. You'd be wasting your time unless you want to be a professor." I think the apostles followed Jesus because they wanted to watch him work.

(4) Hold people accountable. Good mentoring doesn't start by hugging, but by listening, observing, and then challenging. We generally hug too quickly and challenge too late. We should first present a challenge and then hug when they do it or at least attempt to do it (even if they fail and want to try again). Ask yourself, "What am I trying to produce, and what does the person need?" Often, we let our own emotional vacuums color our relationships with the people we are trying to mentor. I'm not afraid to say to a young guy, "Hey man, you gotta work on this," or "That *ain't* gonna cut it." When a character flaw or negative personality trait arises, I ask him, "Why do you think you're like that?" I affirm such people when they do or say something remarkable: "Wow, that's incredible!"

Hold yourself accountable by critiquing yourself with your mentors and others. I recently mailed a form that I've used for several years that allows church members, leaders, family, and friends to critique everything from my "performance" to my character.

(5) Give them bite-size things and watch them. Don't give them the whole load—just a part. See what they do with it. It's the parable of the talents—you're going to find out who invests and who hoards. I think one of the reasons why I wind up being asked to mentor or meet with a lot of guys is because it pays off. They've seen consistency and growth in specific areas that continue to open more and more doors. That happens when you are faithful with the two talents you've been given, not wishing you were a ten-talent guy. The point is not how many talents you have, but how you invest them.

I can see this principle at work in my own life. I'm not a well-known guy, but I'm very well connected. You get that either by being well-known or by being a good producer, and it continues to put you in unique places where a lot of people aren't. The key has been tackling what is in front of me as if it was the only thing, no matter how big or small it is. What you are doing today is often a taste of what is to come, or what could be, if you will learn all you can from it.

(6) Watch what's unique about others and help them discover their own uniqueness. Bob Buford has helped me with this. He has challenged me on more than one occasion, "Roberts, you have to know what is unique about yourself and focus on that. What is it you can do that no one else can?" As I've visited interns in the past on various issues, I see more and more of their

unique giftings. And sometimes I can see something that, left unchecked, was going to hurt them. Or I saw that their true giftedness was somewhere else. I didn't tell them directly or right away what I saw. Instead, I asked questions and planted seeds for their own self-discovery. They value their own discoveries much more than what someone else hands to them! A good mentor blurts out the teaching point only as a last resort.

(7) *Let them see who you really are.* Admit your faults. They already know them and can see them. They aren't asking you for help because they think you're perfect. When you're honest about your weaknesses, you will increase your credibility with them. Let them see you at work, but also let them see you laugh, weep, sweat—everything you are.

One of the men who greatly impacted my life has also made a bad mistake. Why do I still listen to him? Because he picked up the phone and called me before it was in the papers or someone else called. He said, "Bob, I blew it. I love you and believe in you. I'm sorry I've let you down, but I wanted you to hear it from me. This is what happened …" Though I was hurt and disappointed and for a while somewhat confused over the situation, this man to this day speaks deeply into my life. Why? Because he's real. I trust real people—people whose smiles or affirmations aren't mixed with agendas or self-profit.

Recently I spoke with a seventy-three-year-old former pastor named Paul Powell. He likes to refer to himself as a country preacher, but he's no country preacher. He gave me a good "Baptist preacher" outline about avoiding burnout:

1. I am not invincible. I can get sick, sin, and weary.
2. I am not immortal. I am going to die.
3. I am not indispensable. The kingdom keeps going without me.
4. I am not an island. I need friends around me.

Bob: Paul, do you deal with this stuff?
Paul: I've been in the ministry over fifty years and always did.
Bob: Do you ever deal with it today?
Paul: You bet—sometimes it's so hard I fear I won't go on.
Bob: How do you keep going and prevent burning out?
Paul: I'm more sensitive to it today than ever. I used to live in denial—not anymore.

One thing about exceptional leaders is that most arrived in their late forties to mid fifties. It makes sense when you think about it, because it takes a lifetime of learning in order to not just be successful but to impact culture and life. We can only do that if we learn from our mistakes.

August 7
STAND ON MY SHOULDERS
Blog posted by Bob Roberts Jr.

Last fall our last child, Jill, would be leaving in a week to start her freshman year at Baylor University. It made me happy for her, yet sad because I would miss her being at home. I had to work in Orlando, Florida a few days before she left. Since I'd never taken her to Disney World, she persuaded me to take her and her mom with me and in the evenings we'd all play. I got finished with my meetings one night and high-tailed it to the Magic Kingdom. I met them just in time to walk over to the castle and wait for the parade and fireworks. It was awesome! As it began, little kids who were crowded behind others would say, "I can't see, Daddy! I can't see!" Like a great wave, I watched Dads throughout the crowd put their sons and daughters on their shoulders.

I asked Jill, "Can you see?"

Her reply, "No, Daddy."

My reply, "Move over a little!"

I realized then how important this was not just from a father's perspective and his daughter, but from the perspective of an older pastor to a younger pastor. I realized this is the true job of a parent — to get their kids up on their shoulders so they can see farther and more than the parents have or ever will. That's good parenting. But it's also good mentoring. If you have little kids, put them on your shoulder tonight and tell them, "You're taller than me now — tell me everything you see." Then slowly move in a circle. Think about it.

The New Math

$$Bf \times ge + BP = AF$$

An apostolic father is one who equips people and then sends them out. He is generally a broken father (Bf) — someone who has lived long enough and suffered enough to do the right thing with the moral and emotional fiber to see it through. His giving (g) nature is based on his eternal (e) perspective. Because apostolic fathers are highly visionary, you must add to that his big picture (BP) of the kingdom, and you have a formula for an apostolic father (AF).

Chapter 6

DAREDEVIL SONS AND DAUGHTERS

E3 + M + D = CP

Sam was an introvert. Before I met him, I would have questioned anyone who said an introvert can plant a church. How would someone like that get it done? What would compel someone who seemed so shy to persevere and go get the people? Yet Sam did it. Under Sam Carmack's leadership, the first church we ever started—Bear Valley Community Church in Colleyville, Texas—grew to over six hundred people strong. Because of the DNA we imparted to this church, Sam started several other churches as well. He has given more insight to church planters in practical and managerial matters than anyone I know.

Whenever I'm asked what I look for in a church planter, I remember what Sam taught me. He is an example to me that there is no one particular profile that a church planter must fit. I even think it's dangerous to say someone can't plant because they're not "this" or "that." They come in all shapes and sizes. However, they're all daredevils at heart.

I grew up in deep east Texas. In my youth I never smoked and never drank. I was "morally upstanding." It wasn't the things the Bible said I shouldn't do that gave me problems. It was what the Bible didn't say anything about—and I did those kinds of things all the time. I remember one night I was sitting around with a bunch of my buddies, bored out of our minds as we often were in a small town, when we came up with a brilliant idea. What would happen if we turned an old car hood upside down, welded a chair on it, hitched it to the back of one of our pickups with a long metal chain, and "skied" our way down Interstate 20?

We soon found out.

Three at a time, we loaded onto the hood, gave the thumbs-up signal to my buddy who was driving, and took off down a remote section of the interstate just outside our town. Three fat guys from East Texas, too dumb to know better, were having the time of their lives perched on top of an inverted car hood skiing down the highway. Everything was going well until we reached Jim Hogg Road exit and saw a state trooper driving ahead. Before the officer could see us, my buddy quickly turned the wheel and steered into the grassy median. (Ironically, my buddy is now a highway patrol officer.) Still managing somehow to keep us on board, the pickup tore through the grass, narrowly missing a large pole. Unfortunately, our hood did not have power steering, and we careened into the pole, scattering like bowling pins across the grass. We were bruised and bloody, but like the kids we were, we were ready to go again.

How in the world could you ever explain the thrill of going down the interstate on a spark-covered car hood, laughing your guts out with your best buddies? You can't. It's something you have to experience. This is the kind of heart-stopping thrill that church planters live for—they know it's risky, but they don't realize just how risky it is. And it's probably good that they don't. They're daredevils deep inside and there isn't anything they won't try for the sake of the gospel. Beyond that unflagging spirit of courage, most of them possess other skills and traits that lead to transformation.

A Church Planter Profile

In the new math for multiplying churches, I use a formula to describe a church planter (E3 + M + D = CP). Church planters (CP) are entrepreneurial, evangelistic, and equipping (E3), as well as mystics (M) who have learned to observe and reflect, and are creative, on-the-spot designers (D). But before I delve into this profile, a word of warning: don't look for perfection. I don't want church planters who aren't living the Christian life. I am concerned about their prayer life and their practice of personal disciplines. When North-Wood interns start their internship, one of the first things they do is journal about the Sermon on the Mount. I want their lives to come in line with what Jesus expects and learn to emulate him.

Many of us view sin as individual acts of transgression. The Sermon on the Mount gets beyond individual acts to the core—what a follower of Jesus really looks like. During this process, we have had to deal with every imaginable issue regarding our church planters. By virtue of what a planter is like—aggressive, visionary, passionate—they can be especially susceptible to the sins of either pride or self-indulgence. We've had to deal with them at the point of finances, pornography—you name it. I don't look for perfection. I do look for people who are passionate about following Jesus.

Entrepreneurs: The First Ones to Jump

No vocational ministry requires more self-initiating skills than that of church planting. First and foremost, this is what church planters must be if they are going to survive. These are the dreamers—the ones who see something no one else does. They want to get out there and try it. The key characteristic I'm looking for isn't as much success or failure as it is the potential that drives them.

Church planters are visionaries who lead people to accomplish great things. They not only see the vision for themselves; they get others to see it as well. It causes them to be the kind of risk takers that others want to stand alongside. They are the kind of risk takers who compel people to jump with them off a cliff of adventure—all the time reeling and laughing as they're going over the edge. These are the adventurers who love thrills and get a high going up a mountain—especially one that people say is impossible to climb. They are the first ones crossing a desert or bungee jumping off the Empire State Building.

> **Blog posted by Bob Roberts Jr.**
> **September 21**
>
> Not long ago, someone wanted to know my "missiology." I said, "It's simple. Just grab what God has put in front of your face." We want to be missional. We study it and desire it. Yet, I don't know that's what will get us there. Instead, missional is the way we live.
>
> Anyone who knows me knows that I love God and want to see this world transformed. But, today I awoke in North Richland Hills, Texas. Today, I must be missional right where I am. Today, I have to recognize God's face in every situation and every person. Great opportunities to change the world may come today, but they won't come from the other side of the world, they'll come from here. Often people say, "You don't have to go to the other side of the world to be missional." How right they are! God brings it to us right where we are. We then have the luxury, opportunity, or whatever you want to call it, to obey Him here or over there, whatever the case may be. Keep in mind, time and boundaries are not God's. Issues like those are ours.
>
> Let me give you steps on how to be missional that I learned from a man in the Middle East who became a believer on his own by reading the Bible. He literally has only a handful of believers

near him and none of them are Western! These will work for your life, and they will also work for your church.

First, seek God.

Second, obey God.

That's too easy isn't it? Where's the action plan? Where's the purpose statement? Which values line up? Those two steps encapsulate how people are transforming their spaces. The biggest problem with grabbing what's in front of our face is that it doesn't pass through our grid of purpose, values, priorities, goals, and action plans. I live by those things, or I'd go crazy. Too much comes my way. However, I've also learned that my plans are not always God's plans. I'd better have some filter for letting God get through, or I can't do my action plan and fulfill God's plan. God's thoughts and ways are not mine.

I don't want to write about this too much. It may take too much time. Instead, I should be out and about engaging it! I think we have enough literature. We need more stories. Oh yeah, that's the big talk now, as well. We live in a narrative culture. Therefore, we write and lecture on narrative, but what's our narrative!?

... Here comes the ball. Focus on it. Run toward it. Jump up. Reach your hands out. Grab it! Run, baby, run.

Or:

Here comes the ball. Study the ball. Notice the shape and dimensions of the ball. Observe the spiraling patterns. Notice the speed. Map out wind currents and evaluate what the perfect atmosphere is. Look at where it's coming from to understand its origins. Map out projections of the ball. Log all your projections and give lectures on it. Get hit in the head with the ball — what careless person threw that ball?!

An entrepreneur is going to grab that ball like no one else.

Evangelists: Great Conversationalists for Christ

I know few church planters who are not personal evangelists. The kind of evangelist today is very different from what the evangelist was just thirty years ago.

Apologetics is not just the domain of a few intellectuals who write books to give to your coworker or to a neighbor who questions God's existence.

Apologetics represent the necessary understanding of every single person who is sharing his or her faith. Richard Dawkins, Daniel Dennett, and Sam Harris are popular writers who are also scientists—all saying there is no God. Michael Gullion and Francis Clark, however, are the two greatest apologists for Christianity around and both are scientists.

Evangelism is a process that will take time and reflection versus a one-shot presentation, as we often do in the West. Church planters who understand this know that evangelism must move from an event to a process. This is part of the reason why exceptional evangelists are also awesome conversationalists—not people who give others "mysermon.com." They are able to listen to people and craft the conversation around the person instead of the presentation.

In the past, evangelism was a quick presentation and a moment when someone prayed the sinner's prayer. Evangelism is going to have to slow down and become an ongoing conversation with people. Although heaven and hell are real, they are not the starting point of this conversation—Jesus is. In the past, even the way we shared our faith could be interpreted to make consumers out of new Christians. In this newer type of evangelism, prayer and the Holy Spirit are going to be more important.

Equippers — Skillful Encouragers Who Challenge and Coach

Equippers are *teachers of information.*	They know God's Word and can teach it. They can also teach other information that is necessary and appropriate.
Equippers are *trainers of skills.*	They have the ability to help me in what I am trying to do.
Equippers are *motivators—encouragers.*	They challenge me to do more and be more than what I think I can do and be.
Equippers are *coaches.*	They help me with my position and they know the right plays to call at the right times.

Mystics — Seeing and Thinking in Ways Others Don't

Some sociologists say that we are living in the most spiritual time in the history of the United States since before the Civil War. Christians would debate that—but they would lose; it really is the most spiritual time. The problem is that people just don't look to the church and Christianity for spirituality. They delve into New Age or other things. The church is viewed as religious, but not spiritual. Pastors are often seen as preachers taking conservative moral positions—but that's about all.

The greatest compliment someone can give a pastor or church planter is a question. Not, "How did you grow your ministry so I can grow mine?" but rather, "How can I know Jesus as well as you do?" The greatest thing someone can say about another pastor is, "There goes a man or woman of God."

Following God has become too mechanical for too many pastors and not mystical enough. Their disciplines of prayer, journaling, and worship are falling woefully short. People want to be around people who have a natural, living link with God. Often on Sundays, I'll announce something like, "I'm so glad you're here. You may be just checking out the whole God thing. Hope you liked the music, the message, and the atmosphere. However, know this: You can get better music in downtown Fort Worth at the Bass Hall than here. You can get better video clips online or at the movie theater. But we have one thing that we are offering you here today that no one and nothing can match—and that's Jesus."

I'm not afraid of offending nonbelievers by having everyone get on their knees in a service or just asking people to be quiet and listen to what Jesus is saying. People want to listen to those who first and foremost seem to hear from God and "get" spirituality—at least postmoderns do.

Two qualities set apart mystics—the first is observation. Do you hear God's voice? Can you hear it in a song on the radio or in a movie theater in a line of the script? Not long ago my wife and I went to hear B. B. King. Afterward, we were walking in downtown Fort Worth and I said to my wife, "How can people hear a man play like that and not believe there is a God?"

Do you see God in nature? Do you see God in someone hurting? Do you see God in a hungry child's face? He is around us, but most of us don't recognize him. I see signs of God everywhere. I see him in the Buddhist monks trying to find release from a world of suffering. He is at work there, desperately wanting to reveal himself. I see him in the young couple on the motorbike in love clinging to each other as if they're about to die. I see it in a flower bed dividing two roads cluttered with dirt, bikes, trash, and people. A mystic sees things differently.

The other quality that sets a mystic apart is reflection. We gain this quality from being alone, getting quiet, and reflecting. Reflection is prayer—but not always the kind of prayer that is talking; it is listening prayer. Reflection is the missing element of a busy pastor today, but it is essential nonetheless. We have plans, programs, and lots of "stuff" to do, yet we fail to realize that God's work has to be done in his way. Journaling has become a mainstay to me—it's a catalog of reflections. When I pray, I meditate on God's Word; Then I reflect—it's then that I can hear.

Designers—Learning from a World of Knowledge

Designers have learned how to think. These are the guys who can analyze things and see them for what they are. They get the big picture and start putting the pieces together. There was a time when the sharpest person in the community was the pastor. Not anymore. The day of picking a model and following it to a T, expecting that it will get you where you want to be, is over. Things are happening so fast and communities are changing so much that even the model you design today will have to be redesigned and reengineered tomorrow.

These church planters are cross-disciplinary learners. They don't just read religious books; they're into science, novels, sports, and business. Our best learning takes place when we begin to learn outside our own field.

Learning to think is critical. Why? First, God is creative and is always doing a new thing. We can wind up feeling old and useless like a retired athlete when our "methods" and "day" have passed. But if our ministry is more than our methods, we'll be okay. God does a new thing to keep it fresh, and that's good. Isaiah 43:18–19 says, "Forget the former things; do not dwell on the past. See, I am doing a new thing! Now it springs up; do you not perceive it? I am making a way in the desert and streams in the wasteland."

Second, we must learn to think because of the pace of change. Knowledge after World War II was doubling every fourteen years, then seven years, then three years. It's now down to doubling every eighteen months—we have to learn to think in new ways.

Third, there is no set equation in any situation—every situation is unique and has its own parameters. What you knew before may no longer apply.

Fourth, learning to think is what everyone else does whom you will be leading. They have to think daily like this at their jobs.

There were three questions that I had to learn to ask. First was, "How many?" This is a question of quantity. It's what I call level-one thinking. It is basic cause-and-effect information processing. The primary response at this level is to mimic. You hear something works for someone else and you try it. You learn in groups and from practitioners. It's how a baby learns to walk—essential to one's development, but not a good stopping point.

The second question is "Who?" This is a question of identity. Who are the players and the people I'm trying to impact? At this point, you experiment and research. Level-two thinking comes into play and your primary response comes from interacting. You learn alone and from respondents.

The third question is "Why?" It is a question of meaning. In level-three thinking, we integrate what we are learning and evaluate it. Our primary response is to interpret the data. We learn both alone and from primary sources.

To be a designer today, we are going to have to know God—intimately and historically. We must also know ourselves and our communities. Designing doesn't mean just creating the model; it also means developing the plan. The first step in a ten-step process is easy. So is the next step, and the final step. It's steps three through nine that we have to work the hardest on.

Where Is the "L"?

Some may notice something absent from the formula. I've said that church planters (CP) are entrepreneurial, evangelistic, and equipping (E3); mystics (M) who have learned to observe and reflect; and creative, on-the-spot designers (D).

However, some point out that there's no "L" for leadership. Does that mean leadership isn't a trait? Is it something I don't care about? Not at all. I actually believe that these other five traits determine who leaders are and what they will do. It is my definition of a leader in a new church, although these are habits practiced not just by leaders, but by leaders of leaders.

Leadership involves inspiring people to accomplish something significant together that they could never do alone—exactly what a church planter does. You're not just looking for a church planter, but for potential movement leaders.

> Blog posted by Steve Addison
> Australia
>
> 1000 New Aussie Churches, Who's In?
>
> Wondering what it would take to plant 1000 new churches in the Great South Land ...
>
> White hot faith
>
> Commitment to a cause
>
> Contagious relationships
>
> Rapid mobilization
>
> Adaptive methods

I used to think that the measure of leadership was tied to your ability to do things. Great leaders did great things—those who are not-so-great leaders did not-so-great things. This was when the personal impact of my Western individualistic and narcissistic superstardom culture was at its height. In the past, being a great preacher or building a big building or doing something worthy of mention meant a person was a great leader. Drucker got it early on—it had to be more than "charismatic" leadership. He drew examples from Stalin and Hitler, whom he called perhaps the two most charismatic leaders of the twentieth century!

Leadership, particularly that of a pastor, is not tied to one's ability to do great things but to mobilize people (in the context of community) to do more than they could do alone. And more than they ever could have dreamed possible.

December 5

PASTORAL LEADERSHIP IN THE MISSIONAL CHURCH

Blog posted by Bob Roberts Jr.

Pastors that I've been interacting with and teaching for a good while now are mobilizers of the body of Christ to help every part engage society where they touch it. I've been thinking of metaphors of leadership. I think the one I like the most is that of a conduit, or a connector. Our job is nothing less than to know God's Word, our context, people, and opportunities and to connect them. I believe the more we connect them, the more that flows through us. This is the only explanation why God has connected me in so many domains of society and the world. The principle of "faithful in small" and "faithful in much" is the visible expression of connecting. Connecting is so unassuming — just being an outlet for others to pass through. Resources and people and opportunities are like live wires flopping on the floor just waiting to be connected — that's the job of a pastor.

I was recently in a meeting with many exceptional leaders who want to change the world. It's something God put inside all of us. I challenged them that we must be leaders who are bold and gifted, but who also have the ability to be as quiet and as unassuming as a fly on the wall. If we can do that, we'll lead remarkably well and may just have a shot at changing the world.

I recently met a young pastor after a conference who seemed excited, albeit nervous, about starting a new church out of his church. He was in his twenties, just a year or two into his first church of about seventy-five people. Despite his enthusiasm, he kept coming back to the same question, "How will I know when I'm ready?" I think he may have expected me to tell him to get a few years down the road. Or get more resources together and then start later on. I had the feeling that if I had said so, this nervous young pastor may have secretly been relieved!

Instead, I looked him in the eye and told him, *"You're always ready.* There will never be a time when you feel that you have enough money and enough people to do it. In fact, if you don't hurry and do it now, you will never do it."

Obviously, you will be able to do more as you have more resources. However, church leaders need to quit procrastinating and just dare one another to go do it. Today, it's time for you to be a part of starting a new church.

The New Math

E3 + M + D = CP

Church planters are born daredevils — they see it and go for it. They come in every shape and size, but certain common characteristics of planters will result in radical transformation. Church planters (CP) are entrepreneurial, evangelistic, and equipping (E3); they are also mystics (M) who have learned to observe and reflect, as well as creative, on-the-spot designers (D).

Chapter 7

TOTALLY WILD SPIRITS

LCD = D

In China they have a saying: Every believer is a church planter. I agree. The lowest common denominator (LCD) in all church planting is the disciple (D). But I'm often asked, "How do you create disciples like what you are talking about?"

First, I usually tell people who ask me this question to read my first book, *Transformation*, to learn about discipleship that aims at behavior, not just information transfer. The same model, T-Life (transformed life), is being written about by many authors, from Alan Hirsch, author of *The Forgotten Ways*, to Walt Kallestad and Michael Breen, who coauthored *The Passionate Church*. Other churches are practicing it from Jakarta to Beijing, Almaty to Dallas.

Second, I make sure to live it. Until others see it, they'll never get it. I tell our planters all the time, "Until you can stand up and say, 'Imitate me,' as Paul, John, and Peter did, you have no business leading." We've come to believe that if someone can get up and preach, he's ready to go. But if the life doesn't match the message, it becomes destructive.

Third, it's important to understand whom to invest in and how to invest in different people. Also know that the group of men in whom Jesus radically invested for three years were gifted, yet they had their own issues as well.

> Blog posted by Bob Roberts Jr.
> September 21
>
> As pastors, we tend to tie people to religious work, which costs people their time and energy in order to really engage

with those around them. Let me give you an example. I've been taught, and believed until recently, that my job as a pastor was to get everyone somewhere in the five-fold ministry described in Ephesians 4:11: "It was he who gave some to be apostles, some to be prophets, some to be evangelists, and some to be pastors and teachers."

So, what you do is organize the church according to those five ministries and then you have a functioning church. Some people go and initiate ministries (apostles); some challenge us with teaching or obedience (prophets); some evangelize (evangelists); some are the caregivers/nurturers (pastors); some are gifted teachers (teachers). Just find out which of those five areas you put a person in and, if you do that to your whole church, you'll have a functioning church!

No you won't. Show it to me! You can't!

Untaming the Wild

We pastors love those offices and ministries listed in Ephesians 4:11 because they describe who *we* are. These gifts are all rooted in proclamation, and since we have that gift, we tend to have a religious response that pushes our gifts onto others. We've allowed the love of using our gifts to get in the way of others using their own gifts.

In other words, we have tried to turn everyone into preachers instead of salt and light. The world will be won to Christ not because we have more preachers, but because the whole body is being used. We need something big enough to capture their imagination and reintroduce the sense of adventure and risk that is involved in following God.

For too long we have viewed church members as merely the funders of religious work and the volunteers to make Sunday happen instead of the totally wild spirits they really are. How we've approached the person in the pew in the past is insufficient to create a disciple who will be a part of a church multiplication culture. A church that multiplies churches will call on entrepreneurial people to be a part. People who are wild at heart and willing to risk in other areas of their lives come to church and find there's not much adventure here.

You have to develop the desire to take risks to some degree; we're not talking about pure personality traits. But I believe the greatest challenge we face is not making the preacher, pastors, other ministers, and religious vocational workers the heroes, but the typical follower of Jesus. That's the basic job description of a pastor who practices church multiplication: making heroes out of followers of Jesus.

We must raise the whole body to function as salt and light in its daily pattern of living and, in those places, to glorify God. (That's in my next book!) Those offices and ministries exist for those in leadership in the church — not as ends in themselves but as a way of equipping others to do their ministries in engaging society. Read the next two verses in Ephesians: "... *to prepare God's people for works of service*, so that the body of Christ may be built up until we all reach unity in the faith and in the knowledge of the Son of God and become mature, attaining to the whole measure of the fullness of Christ" (Ephesians 4:12 – 13, italics added).

The focus is on how those offices and leaders prepare people so that they can fulfill their ministries — works of service. Those works of service are to be the stuff of sunup to sundown, recognizing God at work — in the family, in relationships — as Rob Bell would say, "making all of life sacred, even sex."

As pastors and leaders, we seem to have come to the tomb of Lazarus and with great authority, passion, and power declared, "Loose him! And let him sit over there!" We have taken off one set of death clothes, only to wrap the person in another set of religious clothes. If we would release people to their own ministries and services in daily life, discipleship would be a daily response to the voice of God. What would that church look like? The lasting results of a church that experiences this kind of transformation are unity, maturity, and fullness.[1]

Interestingly, this culture of personal transformation is something that churches all over the world are practicing and talking about. Many of us have never met one another, and yet we are all saying the same thing. There really is a Holy Spirit. The last time this symmetry happened was during the two Great Awakenings in the United States. Could it be that there is something in the future for us that people have longed to see for millennia? I see the roots of these possibilities even now.

How Do We Lead Them?

It was the first fellowship at our house since all our interns had arrived. We had fifteen young couples of every denominational tradition, background, and race. Adults from their twenties to their forties, representing the countries of Korea, Mexico, Liberia, and the United States, filled our living room. These guys were the cream of the crop, and I was so grateful to be associated with them. We ate barbecue, and then they asked Nikki and me lots of questions — some really good questions. We focused on family a lot and ministry some. Nikki and I shared some stuff and then I opened it up for questions.

Some of them asked me questions about how to lead the people with whom they work. I told them there are five levels of leadership:

Level 1: Leadership by *friendship*:	Since you're my friend, help me, and when you need it, I'll help you as well.
Level 2: Leadership by *systems*:	At 300 people, it's too many people to know everyone well. Mastering infrastructure is crucial.
Level 3: Leadership by *leaders*:	Reproducing yourself and pouring into a few others.
Level 4: Leadership by *vision*:	Though this is present at every level, this is your primary modus operandi and is driven through relationships and systems.
Level 5: Leadership by *leverage*:	Pulling key influencers together to focus one another's energies to do something bigger than they could normally do alone. I'm learning that this is how the "truly greats" have done their greatest work—they live for it.[2] It's movement from the self-centered, self-serving "me" to the other-centered, other-serving "we."

The conversation deepened when the question was raised: "What are we leading them to? What is it you are asking everyone to do?" The answer to this question is critical because the lowest common denominator of church multiplication in local churches is discipleship. What kind of disciple do we have to produce to build church multiplication into the DNA of a new church? How does that disciple look different from a typical disciple in another church?

If a church is going to be a multiplying church, it must focus on the kind of disciple it produces. Discipleship matters here. How do you live out "church"? What do you train disciples to do in "church"? And what is their understanding of their responsibility? All of these issues are crucial.

What Kind of Disciples Do We Need?
Radical: Let Them Do and Be More

Totally wild spirits want to do far more than just serve in a Sunday capacity in their faith. Planters should view Sunday as just on-deck duty for every member and not the essence of their ministry. Each person should have a ministry, but it should be outside the church, not inside. We should all be built up, and we should all be focused out. This is the church unleashed. This is where the church moves and engages all of life, making it possible for change outside the four walls to take place.

How sad that we've settled for a growing campus instead of striving for a transformed community. We've settled for what one person or a small group of leaders can do. A single preacher who is gifted enough in many areas can grow a big campus with his team. However, no preacher is "big" enough to see his community transformed without mobilizing the entire body of Christ into operation. I've learned that the best thing I can do in the community is to saturate it with members of NorthWood because they have more clout, influence, and understanding of how society works than I and most preachers ever will.

Comprehensive: Encourage Them to See Life as a Whole

The Vietnamese painters, under French influence, have taken impressionism to a whole new level. Hanoi has impressionistic art studios and galleries that rival those in any place in the world. I've become friends with many of the painters there and love to watch them work. When people enter our church, they are blown away by the vibrant and dramatic art on the walls. Their first question is, "Where did you get these paintings?"

They are originals from Hanoi. I'm looking at a painting right now of a Red Zao woman. I've admired the painter and his use of colors because he captures something most artists can't when he paints these people. I found out his mother is a Red Zao from Taphin, a section of northern Vietnam where we work. Now this painting has double meaning for us because we know that this artist paints his life into his pictures. They all do. Another friend of mine, Minh Song, paints churches because there was an old Catholic church near a river where he grew up—another example of how these artists' lives go into their art.

Van Gogh was no different. Van Gogh painted his most famous painting, *The Starry Night*, while he looked out an insane asylum to which his brother Theo had committed him for a period. However, the church he paints in the small town below is not there in reality. Neither is it the expected style of a French church but rather that of a Dutch Reformed church—the kind he grew up in. Painters, writers, and artists do not compartmentalize life; it is the source of their inspiration and their goal is the connection of all of that into their art.

The disciple who is the building block of church multiplication does the same thing with faith. That kind of disciple has an all-inclusive walk with God. A personal relationship with Christ engulfs his or her life, family, and vocation and the way he or she relates to society. It does not just go into effect at church. We focus the work of the gospel too little on the whole person. We allow people to stop far too quickly in terms of knowing what it means to follow Christ.

Comprehensive disciples see life as a whole and everything as an opportunity to grow—even when it's painful. They see pain as an opportunity to grow and experience God in deep ways. They see God in who they want to become; they see him in their families; they see him in people.

Vocational: Tell Them How to Use Their Jobs

The disciple who will change the DNA of a church to be a church planting church will view their job or vocation as their number one ministry, not just a way to make a living. They will view their skill or competency as a gift God has given them to be used for his glory. As a result, they will reach people and be agents of the kingdom in places that historically have not been thought of as kingdom places for a long time—at copy centers, pet stores, Wal-Marts, and a million other locations.

Luke 9:23 says, "If anyone would come after me, he must deny himself and take up his cross daily and follow me." What does it mean to take up one's cross and follow Jesus? For each person it is different. The cross is not just a symbol of pain, it's a symbol of redemption. Our jobs are the way that we redeem the world most completely, and we "take them up" every day during the week. If all believers viewed their vocations as their primary ministry, the whole of society would change. Too often we make the "take up your cross" part to be, "sit through this service"!

Intimate: Help Them Love Jesus More

This kind of disciple wants to know God and experience him intimately. Prayer, fasting, service, journaling—all of these things are going to be important to them. The focus is on Jesus and knowing him through the Holy Spirit. He is not going away; there will be no such thing as a person who isn't filled with the Spirit who lives this out.

The greatest thing you can do for a disciple is to teach him or her how to worship personally. We spend so much time planning worship, or even doing it as churches or small groups. But the greatest form of worship is personal worship. It should never stop there with the individual; it should move into community. Yet teaching people to worship changes the whole of who they are. They begin to see God moving and working everywhere. When all hell breaks loose in our families, we can stay calm knowing where the source of our strength is. The worship of God is how we glorify him. The way we know we have worshiped him is not by how we feel, but by the fruit of service that follows.

Servant: Show Them How to Look Outward

Consumerist disciples will never be the kind of leaders a church has to have in order to see people live beyond their expectations. Establishing church plants that transform the community requires raising up disciples who are willing to sacrifice. Jesus gives us the example of servanthood as he goes to the cross.

In John 12:23–26 Jesus says, "The hour has come for the Son of Man to be glorified. I tell you the truth, unless a kernel of wheat falls to the ground and dies, it remains only a single seed. But if it dies, it produces many seeds. The man who loves his life will lose it, while the man who hates his life in this world will keep it for eternal life. Whoever serves me must follow me; and where I am, my servant also will be. My Father will honor the one who serves me." Servanthood says we are more concerned about the needs of others than we are our own personal needs.

Pilgrims: Remind Them It's an Unpredictable Journey

Living life on pilgrimage is a way of living the Christian life in adventure. There is so little adventure in Christianity today for the average follower of Jesus. It's too predictable, too easy, and too pat. It's fun to live the Christian life in such a way that you don't always know the next bend or how the current bend is going to impact you. When you live life on pilgrimage, you are learning to walk by faith — something we don't do a lot of today. It's too predictable.

Disciples who understand this are going to be much more open to not having to have all their questions answered. People don't want a 1-2-3 program; they're longing for adventure and to be a part of something emerging. A missionary goes and gives; a pilgrim not only goes and gives but gets along the way. It's a journey and a process in which everything builds on everything else to lead to something beyond their expectations.

When people start getting excited about walking with God, they realize they can do more to make a difference. Boundaries adjust and they start doing things they never dreamed possible. One man in our church is a police officer who serves as a SWAT team leader. I started taking him with me to Vietnam and then Afghanistan, which really just whetted his appetite. Through a different set of circumstances, he began working with Fulani Muslims in Nigeria, a group of people with historically volatile relationships with Christians. He ended up serving as a stateside mobilizer for Nigeria. He has met key chiefs, tribal leaders, and a good deal of uncertainty along the way.

One night in Nigeria, the car in front of him entered a hail of gunfire. It was a terrifying, terrible scene. Many people lost their lives. But that didn't deter him a bit. Next Wednesday, he's leaving on a plane to return to Nigeria with thirty people to serve in an orphanage, medical center, and local school to be a blessing to the Fulani. The irony is that this SWAT team leader just *thought* he lived on the edge after years in the police force, busting down doors and entering firefights. But what's really getting him juiced up is what he's now doing all around the world for Christ.

King David understood this craving for adventure in Psalm 84:5–7: "Blessed are those whose strength is in you, who have set their hearts on pilgrimage. As they pass through the Valley of Baca, they make it a place of springs; the autumn rains also cover it with pools. They go from strength to strength, till each appears before God in Zion."

Giving: Model for Them What It Means to Give It All

We're going beyond tithes and offerings here. The disciple's giving is driven by a vision of what God is calling them to do. There is nothing greater than giving something that makes a difference and impacts others. How can we followers of Jesus give in such a way that it changes the face of a community?

As I write this, it's a muggy March day in Hanoi, Vietnam. I'm sitting out on the second-floor balcony of the Paris Café on Church Street. It's a street of average width for the neighborhood where I live in North Richland Hills. Yet hundreds of little motorcycles fill the roads as parents pick up their children from a school nearby. Kids are laughing as they put on their helmets. It's just like it was back at Green Valley School where my children grew up. I even see a couple of chunky kids that remind me of Ben and Jill grinning from ear to ear. One is picking his nose, another—well, I can't say! Parents are hugging their kids and the streets are filled with smiles and laughter—just another day in Hanoi and everyone is happy.

They have enough food, a roof over their heads, and jobs, and things are looking up for Vietnam. I realize I'm looking at the future right outside my window. However, I also realize that today, and at least for the next two decades, their opportunities won't be as good as children back in the United States. It doesn't seem fair. Where does the difference lie? Sitting here on the balcony looking below, they seem to have the same family love and the same dreams and aspirations.

In truth, the difference lies in a system and infrastructures—an assembly line that people follow in both societies that leads to two different results. I'm convinced that just preaching that people should love Jesus more will get us nowhere. We must produce disciples who are willing to give themselves to engage at the level of system and infrastructure and begin to make a difference down the road for a future generation they may never know. Consider Pastor John Sharp's story as an example.

A BEAUTIFUL THING

Blog posted by John Sharp, pastor,
North Point Community Church, Columbia, South Carolina

A personal calling is a beautiful thing. Many never discover theirs or never find the place to live it out. I began the journey toward the adventure God called me to live out in 1996. While I was attending seminary, my wife got a job as an administrative assistant at this strange young church called NorthWood. Soon after she started the job, I began to get to know Bob Roberts. Bob told me I would make a great church planter. Every time I saw him, he reminded me that church planting was the greatest thing under the sun. I started sensing a pull to learn more about the process of beginning a new church that multiplies rapidly. God finally persuaded me to join the church planting center at NorthWood, and Bob took me under his wing.

At that point in my life, I was desperately seeking the "one place" God created me to fit in. The mold that only I was shaped to fill. Bob brought me along until I came to the space that I knew I was created to occupy. The space is known as multiplication through church planting. I found it to be true that few are wired and shaped for the calling, and even less actually embrace it. At that time, it was billed as the more difficult path to take. One that only the outcast or jobless choose. In all actuality, it was meant for the brave at heart, the passionate and driven individual that is willing to take a big risk for the kingdom.

Parts of the learning journey were truly inspiring. I was sent to incredible conferences, met important people, and listened to practitioners that were successfully doing what was being taught. I had the opportunity to help several other church planters in the vicinity launch their new work. I was able to learn, see, and help do what God was calling me to do.

Other parts of the learning journey were tiring and monotonous. We literally drove street to street to demographically map neighborhoods and communities. I folded brochures and newsletters and set up chairs. I worked in the lobby and parking lot on Sunday mornings. I made phone calls and ran errands. There was even a time or two when the bathroom needed cleaning. Bob's mantra: "church planters have to do that"! And so it was.

I left Texas to follow God's call for my life in Columbia, South Carolina. My wife, Christie, and I were the first members of the church. We knew no one else in the community and had no ready-made group to help launch this church. I began knocking on neighbors' doors to meet people and build new relationships. We pursued friendships with people we discovered had no relationship with a church. We started a Bible study in our living room that summer, and people miraculously came. In less than three months we outgrew our home, and moved to the atrium of an office building in which a core group member worked. That man became one of our first converts, and is still with us today!

In January of 1999, North Point Community Church (NPCC) was officially launched in a public school with about 75 people. We grew slowly and steadily for 2 years and made a move to the local movie theater. Again we grew slowly and steadily, until the purchase of our first property 3 years ago. At that point God began to add to our numbers quickly, and more people than ever were being baptized at NPCC. I'm excited that we are now one of the leaders in baptism for our area. More than that, I am excited about the multiplication that is taking place.

NPCC has helped plant 4 churches since our inception in 1999. We prayed for and sent finances, sent childcare workers, hung door hangers, threw Frisbees, and gave equipment to guys that were doing what we had done. These guys all had a commitment to do the same after they launch. We will probably be mentoring our first church planter this year in an on-site internship. That launch will be in our own community. I don't want to be the biggest church in the community; I want to reach the community.

In the past year, we are entering the global realm of multiplication. We have always supported missionaries and mission trips abroad, but now we are beginning to take responsibility for a part of the world. I took a trip to North India in 2006 that changed my life. We were there to pray, share Christ, and look for opportunities to partner for multiplication in order to reach the country. The third day of the trip I met a village leader. He invited us into his home to have tea and talk. As we talked, he shared with us he had seen us come to his home in a dream. We were even wearing the same clothes that day as he saw in his dream. I shared my testimony with him, and after we explained the gospel, he trusted Christ. Before we left that day, he gave me a silver ring he was wearing, and I gave him a silver ring I was wearing. I didn't see him again on that trip, but heard of a dream he had the next night. He was handing out water to villagers as they came to his house. A house church pastor explained it was living water that he was giving to his people. I believe another movement of God was birthed in that village!

The things that were passed on to me so many years ago as a young man in Texas are now being passed around the world. The man that soaks up and stores up will become dry and irrelevant. The one that gives away everything that is passed to them will be involved in the greatest movement of all time — multiplying to the ends of the earth!

The New Math

LCD = D

The lowest common denominator (LCD) in all of church planting is the disciple (D).

Chapter 8

START WITH THE SOCIETY, NOT THE CHURCH

$S + C(cc) \times V = CT$

When John Bisagno was pastor of First Baptist Church in Houston, he and the missions pastor, Harvey Kneisel, were starting churches before it was even popular to talk about it. However, their technique was unprecedented. They began by identifying an inner-city church that had run down. They would seed it with their own members and watch it grow again — a different, new plant, but one that was healthy and strong. What has been exciting is that this vision for multiplying churches didn't stop with John. If anything, under the leadership of the new pastor, Gregg Matte, and missions pastor, William Taylor, it's picking up speed.

> Several years ago an inner-city church, Park Temple Baptist Church in Houston, Texas, contacted me with the proposal that we take over their church to see if we could seriously address the needs of their community. Membership was down to about 35 people. Here was a church with a one and a half million dollar property, a sanctuary to seat 700 people, fifty thousand square feet of education space, a bus in the garage, a complete library, a baptistery in place, but not one baptism in years. They were located strategically on a major street and debt free. Could we call ourselves a Great Commission church and turn them down?
>
> Now for the rest of the story. We invited a lay member of First Baptist to become their pastor. A governance committee was put in

place to assist in the transformation. Park Temple now has approximately 200 attendees on a regular basis. But it is a different clientele. The old church consisted of 35 elderly Anglos, but the community was at least 90 percent Hispanic. Now the church is 60% Hispanic, 20% African-American and 20% Anglo and others. They now look just like the community. They have also started a successful Christian school, a Day Care, an ESL program, a bus ministry, and a substance abuse ministry. The baptistery is often used.

Houston's First Baptist has now partnered with 24 dying churches. Three things are apparent when working with transitional churches.

1. God has solved the **space problem**. Most of the churches have 50 to 100 thousand square feet of unused building space. That solves the need of purchasing and erecting a very expensive church plant.

2. God has also solved the **location problem**. No longer do we need to erect facilities on the "wrong side of the track" or on a dead end street to reach our greatest mission field. These seldom-used buildings are located on the busiest traffic lanes of America.

3. God also solved the **finance problem**. Let's face it. Our most difficult problem in starting new churches is getting strategic finances to start new churches and erect new buildings. Our Lord already owns them! And they are paid for in full. They are only waiting for the declining churches to partner with the stronger mission-minded church, who will lead in the process of reaching out to the "new community."

After we had partnered with three dying churches, we invited 55 similar churches to a Saturday brunch. There we expressed our love and concern for their dilemma. We gave examples of how our first three partnerships resulted in growth from 200 to 1500 percent growth in a short period. The next 21 approached us with a request for help. The statistics have not changed. We have seen equal success.

At present I have retired from the staff of Houston's First Baptist Church and am serving as a "Missions Consultant" for their new church starts and declining church transitions. For the last 16 months I have been Interim Pastor of Long Point Baptist Church. This church was also in great decline. The facilities and grounds were also in bad condition. Attendance was around 35. My first Sunday, we had two young people and no children. Membership had been closed to prevent another group from taking over the church and property. It was recently appraised at over $3,000,000.00. Many groups desired it. However, they did not want to reach the community! Since then we have re-addressed the community. Sixty percent of the

"now community" is Hispanic and many are of a much lower socio-economic strata. We came under the "watch care" of Houston's First Baptist Church for a 5-year period to give a serious effort of reaching our community. People are being saved and baptized. The church has graded a Sunday school and a children's ministry. We invited a Spanish-speaking congregation to share our facility. They have at least 220 members on a Sunday and we average more than 70+. This is not the end of the story.

We partnered with a young Vietnamese pastor, David Mai, to start a new mission church in our facility 10 months ago. Within six months they had over 70 members. As they ran out of space, they moved to a new location. Now they have approximately 175 in church each Sunday. What is the bottom line of what God is doing? Now over 400 people have come to or through Long Point Baptist Church in the last 16 months. That is much better than dying! Does that sound like something God would be up to?

There is a unique quality about Filipinos that we need. When they are asked to do a very needy task, some one will invariably come up and say, "I will be the one." We need thousands of other churches who will say, "We will be the one."[1]

Starting Where It Matters

Harvey's story reminds us that it's not about church planting but about the transformation of society. I love that story because it's about a traditional church getting it right. If you don't nail this, you'll waste so much time. If it's just about starting a church and the Sunday event, then you can trash this chapter. If it's just about baptizing a bunch of people a year, then you can do that and forget about doing what I'm challenging you to do.

However, the principle of "starting with society and not the church" matters more to church multiplication than anything else you're going to read. Without an understanding of this key point, it's possible to do churches, buildings, converts, baptisms, programs, mission work, and inner-city work—and still see your community degenerate. If, however, you want to see radical transformation, then read on.

Until a few years ago, had you asked me what the church existed to do, I would have told you, "to get as many converts as possible." That's not good enough. We've been called to make disciples and bring life and hope. As I began to read the Sermon on the Mount and to follow the ministry of Jesus, I couldn't escape what he did and how he engaged the poor and hurting. Then I began to study Israel and her purpose of existence and realized how off base I had been. If I focus on getting converts, I only make people more religious. If I focus on societal transformation, converts are a must, but now I'm defining what the true focus is: *mobilizing the whole church to engage the whole society to see the community transformed.*

The biggest challenge for church planters today is to realize they are to start with the society, not the church. "Church" planter or "church" starter may not be the best term to describe what we really want to happen. Perhaps "community faith engager" is a better term than church planter. Church planters should think like community developers more than anything else. They go into a community to scout out everything and then get to work.

Nehemiah is a beautiful example of this principle in motion. He goes in and quietly studies before he starts anything. He knows where the gates are down and then organizes people according to where they live to begin rebuilding the walls. We need to do the exact same thing today.

In the past few decades, the process for starting churches has been predictable (see Figure 12). It begins with an organization, network, or denomination identifying a community that needs a church. Next, they find a church planter. He starts the church, and as it gets bigger, ideally the church starts engaging the community. Down the line, maybe they will help plant another church. In this model, the church comes before the society.

Institution → Gospel → Preacher → Church → Society → Institution → Planting

Figure 12: Traditional Model for Starting Churches

In contrast, here's the Acts 11 model of how churches were started (see Figure 13). We start with the gospel, pure and simple. It finds its way to a disciple. The disciple begins to change from the inside out. He or she lives it and engages people wherever they are in society. From there, the church emerges. This church is evangelistic — and it doesn't have a program. Evangelism is what this church is, not something it tries to promote and do. In this model, engaging the society comes first; then comes the church.

Gospel → Disciple → Society → Church

Figure 13: Acts 11 Model for Starting Churches

Think Like a Community Developer

To start a church that starts with the society, the church planter must think and act like a community developer, not just a preacher. You have to know how a society comes together. The building blocks of societies are specific domains or infrastructures, such as education, health care, government, law, and the like.

Believe it or not, God has put societies together in line with his kingdom. Community building is not a new idea; it's as old as civilizations. You have to know these domains of society and what is going on in each one (see Figure 14).

Figure 14: Domains of Society

Often the society will determine the actual work of the church in a community because of the needs of a particular domain. In the past, the church would pick something to focus on randomly. But now the mission is obvious because it's where the church already is. The primary place of ministry becomes a specific domain in society, not the church on the corner. The template for reaching society isn't a list of people you are going to try to witness to, but those around whom you already live your life on a daily basis.

How does the gospel intersect a society? Through believers serving in domains, the building blocks of a society. How do churches emerge? Relational services (facilitated by believers' jobs) impact various domains, and the people in these domains begin to follow Christ. These Jesus followers result in organic churches (see Figure 15).

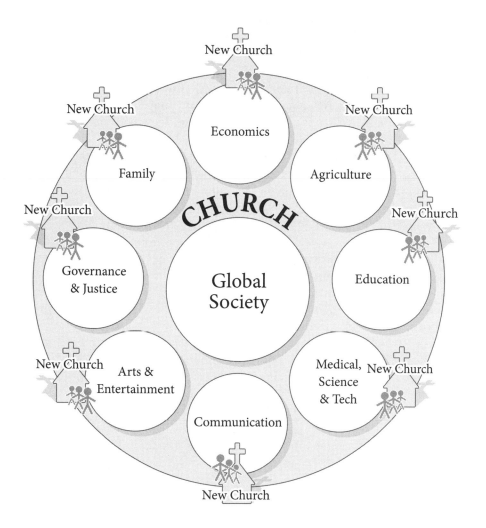

Figure 15: The Church as a Connection Center

Unfortunately, churches have not thought in terms of engaging domains but instead often think in terms of traditional missional approaches. David Watson, speaking of geography and domains, once said, "People don't realize they are living on borders of the kingdom of heaven and there are no walls that they have to choose to walk across borders."

Globalization has changed everything. This template is not just how you engage your community but also how you engage the world. Every society in every nation uses similar infrastructures. If you follow this, you don't just get a map for your community, you get a map for the world.

Pick a Spot, Any Spot

To start a church that starts with the society, you have to identify where to jump in from day one. It's similar to they way you would typically do a demographic analysis of a particular community. How many people live there? How many churches are there? Focus on what is going on in the communities in each domain. Where is the biggest challenge? How will we first engage? That is going to determine the disciples you reach at first.

Starting a church is also determined by who is in your church. God is already at work in the society; what you are doing is adding salt and light to darkness and decay. What kind of salt and what kind of light do you have in your church? What vocations are represented? What skill sets and experiences do your members have that are useful in a particular domain?

Tremendous opportunities exist locally and globally for a church to exhibit the kingdom of God in domains where the members have vocational skills or passions. Churches that don't have a clear picture of the skills, talents, giftings, passions, and vocations of their members will never get to this step. Churches that don't know what opportunities exist in what regions or domains cannot effectively connect their people.

However, once you "get it," you realize you have opened the potential of starting multiple churches out of multiple domains. In the past, we thought of church planting first in terms of geography. Then we thought in terms of psychographics. Now we must start thinking in terms of societal engagement — which is what we should have been doing all along. Had we been doing that, we would have gotten geographically dispersed and psychographically diverse at the same time.

A New Day for Discipleship

To start a church that starts with the society, you have to redefine discipleship. Your new focus in discipleship is to connect the entire body of Christ in a community and literally open the church up to ministry. They will dream up the initiatives, and they will implement them. The primary function of the church is then helping people live what they're already interested in doing (because of their job, experience, skills, etc.) more than driving an ill-fitting program. Existing community service organizations are always in need of volunteers and many times already have the funding and network to get things going.

Imagine what doors this could open for new curricula and new church service organizations. Let's dream big. If people start by living as disciples personally and in their families, then engaging their job — watch out. You could wind up with new churches emerging out of an interesting incubator, a domain of society.

The Church as a Connection Center

To start a church that engages the society, the church must become a central place of worship and the hub of connecting to society. Each local church is a connection center. When this happens, the church goes viral. People start owning the ministry and things start happening dramatically. You're going to mobilize the entire church, not just preachers and those in religious vocations. This will also impact how disciples from other churches begin to interact with one another. Other laypeople are not going to wait for their own local churches to provide systems and opportunities to engage society; they are going to start doing it on their own.

It's amazing that people can be successful businesspeople, doctors, lawyers, teachers—everything—yet they have separated their faith from their work. How tragic! Our job must be to help them engage their work. It is happening around the world more and more. Why hasn't it happened sooner?

I believe the institution of the church has been so heavy and the secular and sacred so divided by leaders who don't want to lose their Sunday workforce, that we've failed to help disciples see what they are called to do. They just need some permission and a little push.

I'm often asked why as I pastor I'm so obsessed with engaging the society. The answer is easy. This really is the mission of the church: to mobilize believers to engage every domain of society; to set in motion the radical transformation that the gospel brings to every person and sphere of life. I also believe new churches are the best hope for achieving this mission. This is how the church in Antioch grew. Paul didn't do all this stuff by himself. As a matter of fact, it started without him.

The New Math

$$S + C(cc) \times V = CT$$

Start with the Society (S) when you want to make a difference. Add the church (C)—but add it with each local church being a connection center (cc) for people to connect their jobs with their ministry. Multiply that times the vocations (V) of the membership of the church, and you will get community transformation (CT).

Chapter 9

START A CHURCH FOR THE WORLD

$MC^2 + FP = GC$

Yesterday we commissioned one of our interns who has since headed to Kentucky to plant. He joined us on our annual trip to Vietnam, and it proved to be the perfect opportunity for me to remind him of some central truths. I challenged him never to forget that the church is meant to be far beyond just that one spot where he was going to plant in the Bluegrass State. When we start a church, we realize we are doing so not just for the community but for the world, based out of that community. Every church you start is a church for the world.

Each year when our interns join us on our global projects, most go through some kind of cathartic experience. They've heard me speak about it, but when they see the places for the first time, something happens. I guess I shouldn't be shocked; people like me who have been raised in church hearing the Great Commission are forever changed once they actually go on a mission somewhere.

A strange thing happened at NorthWood. When we agreed as a church to adopt Vietnam, our stateside church planting began to explode. Although we had planted two or three churches over time, the pace suddenly moved to planting one every year, then two a year. Now it has moved to planting more than ten churches a year. I am convinced that when you connect with the big picture of God, all the rest falls in place. Starting a church is the natural response of a living church to its community. Engaging the world is the Father's comprehensive response to a lost world.

When that happens, we are connected with God at a deep level in terms of his will, his mission, and his passion. He begins to multiply what he wants incredibly fast. I challenge you to plant churches that see what the Father sees. If you do, those churches are going to explode.

The Great Tragedy

The great tragedy of American church planting is that it has become about us, our location, and our community. Local churches with the mandate of the Great Commission have instead become the epitome of religious institutional consumerism. The multiplying gene of a new church is not just one piece of the new math in church multiplication. Multiplication is comprehensive and moves into the whole will of God, the whole realm of society, and the whole span of the globe. This is a DNA that moves out.

In the same way that each new church plant is required to start another new church plant in its first year, we require new church plants to adopt a nation and begin working there. We are simply setting the DNA of that new church to look at the potential of the community and the world. During the first year of working in that nation, all they may do is pray and send their pastor and a layperson. The layperson is important because otherwise we end up doing what we pastors do — religious work.

An Antioch Strategy

Now those who had been scattered by the persecution in connection with Stephen traveled as far as Phoenicia, Cyprus and Antioch, telling the message only to Jews. Some of them, however, men from Cyprus and Cyrene, went to Antioch and began to speak to Greeks also, telling them the good news about the Lord Jesus. The Lord's hand was with them, and a great number of people believed and turned to the Lord.

News of this reached the ears of the church at Jerusalem, and they sent Barnabas to Antioch. When he arrived and saw the evidence of the grace of God, he was glad and encouraged them all to remain true to the Lord with all their hearts. He was a good man, full of the Holy Spirit and faith, and a great number of people were brought to the Lord.

Then Barnabas went to Tarsus to look for Saul, and when he found him, he brought him to Antioch. So for a whole year Barnabas and Saul met with the church and taught great numbers of people. The disciples were called Christians first at Antioch.

Acts 11:19 – 26

The church in Jerusalem was a gathering church for all the people accepting Christ in that community. Once persecution came, they dispersed. However, notice that those people who were tied in some way to the deacon Stephen began to go to work. Paul had not yet been given all his revelations about including the Gentiles. The church didn't know anything about church planting. But look what happens—these laypeople had connections with fellow businessmen and tradesmen and others in their circle of influence. They began to share the good news with Gentiles, and the Gentiles responded to it. It was the gospel, pure and simple, without the Judaism that the laypeople had been raised with. This is why it created concern and caused the apostles to send Barnabas to check it out.

Fascinating. The first church outside of Jerusalem that we have record of did not start a church by religious decree. Theirs was not an intentional response of the church in Jerusalem to plant churches and spread the gospel. Instead, the seed of the gospel left Jerusalem soil, scattered, and took root on its own in Antioch. It grew and then immediately spread to Asia Minor. This passage proves my theory about a Jesus movement because that's all it was—a Jesus movement. There was no strategy or formula or long-range plan to plant churches.

The mission is simple cause and effect. Those who function in a particular domain of society live the gospel powerfully and other people want it. As a result, churches form to (1) teach those who have been birthed from evangelism and (2) mobilize the church to engage the world. Wow! What if we started churches like that today? Do you see the difference? Today we start churches and then do evangelism to reach people. What if churches were birthed out of evangelism as in Antioch? I believe we'd have a radically different kind of church. This is what we are seeing in China and other parts of the world.

I believe the offices and organization of the church are important and should be kept and maintained. I also believe local congregations can emerge without "positional," trained leaders from the outside. Leadership can come from among the believers who are meeting. If this weren't possible now, it never would have been possible for the church to spread as it did then. This is one of the reasons I'm involved with Vision360 and am so excited about it. It is a church planting network with a movement mentality that is driven by Al Weiss, the layman I mentioned in chapter 3. This is a first. It is not focused on your typical religious personnel starting churches.

Not Paul's Idea

Notice in Acts 13 that missionaries aren't sent out from Jerusalem, the base of faith. Instead, they're sent out from Antioch. Also notice that they aren't sent because they had a "personal" call, but they were sent at the insistence of laypeople in the church. These laymen, who had become prophets and teachers, were in a prayer meeting when they felt led to have Barnabas and Saul/Paul hit the road to spread the message. There is no indication that Paul and Barnabas were even thinking about moving in that direction. However, the church at Antioch realized how easily the gospel was spreading in Greek culture.

> In the church at Antioch there were prophets and teachers: Barnabas, Simeon called Niger, Lucius of Cyrene, Manaen (who had been brought up with Herod the tetrarch) and Saul. While they were worshiping the Lord and fasting, the Holy Spirit said, "Set apart for me Barnabas and Saul for the work to which I have called them." So after they had fasted and prayed, they placed their hands on them and sent them off.
>
> Acts 13:1–3

The whole story of Acts from this point forward is only possible because the gospel (first planted in Jerusalem) outgrew its pot when persecution broke out! The seedling then became a vine, not a little plant, and began spreading with power and force. Now that the vine began following the sun (Son) toward Asia Minor, the entire church started getting involved. The story of Acts isn't tied to a single person but to a church bent on moving a global movement forward. This is a DNA beyond personality and hype.

DECONSTRUCTIONISM VERSUS DENIAL

Blog posted by Bob Roberts Jr.

Churches that are constructed from new believers in "virgin" nations (with reference to the gospel) have a combustible mix of excitement, enthusiasm, miracles, persecution and difficulties — all happening simultaneously. There is no question that the West is a postmodern culture. With postmodernism comes deconstructionism that allows us to strip away nonessential layers built up over time that actually encumber the spread and power of the gospel. Maybe some of those layers were good for a certain time and place. However, as time and places change, they become more of a hindrance than a blessing.

Deconstruction is sometimes necessary. It means going back to the original to rebuild for a unique generation. But there is a problem when it goes far beyond that, denies who God made us to be, and minimizes someone's faith.

When we begin to deconstruct, we often disregard what God did and how he worked in one era. It's the tendency to place one's own time and space on a pedestal in contrast to others. That can lead to arrogance of opinion that makes us feel as though our methodology is superior. It can even lead to anger and resentment over the bondage that the past may have brought with it. This kind of response will *never* allow someone to successfully reinvent the church for their era.

Len Sweet has made a huge contribution to the church by describing the "ancient future." No one is considered more "future" and "edgy" than Sweet — yet he never trashes what has been. He always challenges what can be. I remember sitting with him one time during a meeting where people were clearly caught in a time warp. I have to admit I was somewhat embarrassed. So, I leaned over and said to him, "I'm sorry, man, you can see how much we need help!" He just smiled and said, "Don't deny your roots — this is what has enabled you to be where you are." His way of pushing me forward has always been to build on the past, not rip it. Good advice.

Defining the Core Group

Defining the core group involves a creative tension between having to take off the old layers, but doing it with an attitude of grace and gratitude. Maybe you do so by celebrating each layer (era) and remembering what the family was like at that stage. The privilege of being around first-generation Christians in some nations allows me to see the emergence of the virgin church. What I've seen is incredible enthusiasm and excitement over constructing something to reach their society. I have yet to see happy, vibrant, movement churches emerge from deconstructionism. I'm convinced that the church will spread rapidly only when people are excited and enthused, and evangelism is naturally and aggressively taking place.

This is why one of the best hopes of reaching people in the West is the house church movement. Effective house church movements, however, are not going to come from frustrated "religious professionals" who have given up on church in one form to adopt another. Nor will they come from frustrated people who are angry at the established church. Only those who are excited and in love with Jesus can gather and attract similar others.

Talk about the issue is important because the core group of a new church is going to do more to determine the future of that church than anything else. I've seen it too many times—a core group of established Christians with an ethos of reinvention leads to one church. Reaching people without Jesus and letting the enthusiasm of new believers reach other people in that category will yield a totally different church plant, and it applies to house, contemporary, postmodern—all types of plants.

Unique Features of a Global Church

A global church sees the church as the missionary and the laypeople as the missionaries. For this to work, you have to raise up disciples who live it and love it, spread it and share it. The whole church gets involved in the game this way. As in Antioch, the enthusiasm for the movement is driven not by the preachers but by the people who are following Jesus.

A global church engages the whole of society. It goes back to starting with the society and engaging the domains of society as opposed to starting with religious work.

A global church is one that is planting churches locally and globally. The action takes place simultaneously, not "first do one and then the other." Each culture, as Chuck Kraft has noted, represents a different pot in which to plant the seed of the gospel. Therefore, planting methodologies and approaches need to be driven from within the field, not from the West. Partnering with churches around the world is always a good thing. Just be sure that they are partners in every sense of the word and that they, not you, are driving your church planting strategy.

In some places, you cannot plant the church legally. What about them? My experience around the world confirms that a church in the West doesn't need to worry about that. The Antioch strategy has been happening all over the world since the first Antioch happened. It will be implemented not by outsiders but by insiders who grab it and run. When someone or something plants the seed of the gospel in someone on the inside of an illegal country, you have a church planter. It goes beyond anything that books write about—and it happens all the time.

A global church makes a long-term transformational commitment to a specific place in the world until that specific place also becomes a sending place. It is hard for a new church to engage the world. It was for us, and it will be for others. Often I'm challenged at the point of getting a church to focus on a specific spot long term. However, the American church has spent billions of dollars on mission trips that have bebopped around the globe with little to show for it. Only work that is invested over time will make a significant impact.

Where Will a Global Church Planting Movement Emerge?

Trying to predict where a global church planting movement will emerge is dangerous pseudoscience. I'm always reminded of what Isaiah wrote about God, "My thoughts are not your thoughts, neither are your ways my ways" (Isaiah 55:8). However, there is one thing I can say with great confidence, and it doesn't take a futurist to recognize it: a global church planting movement will come from the East.

We have technology—they have the Spirit.

We have processes—they have hearts.

We have money—they have faith.

We have plans—they have results.

Beyond that, I would say the most likely places where a global church planting movement will occur will be "flat places" where everyone can come along. Movements begin with affinity—ethnicity being the primary one in the past twenty years. If a movement is going to break out of affinity, we must identify the most obvious global connection points that cross all societies and nations. Here we have ripe conditions for the emergence of a global church planting movement. The following are examples of the most obvious flat places—but please keep in mind that it will probably come from a future setting that I haven't even listed!

Cities

The spread of the gospel has historically always been tied to the cities. From there it spreads out across the rest of the world. Cities are linked in almost every way. In two thousand years, there has never been a church planting movement that has come from the countryside.

Domains

The way society is put together causes people to connect with one another across nations, ethnicities, and even languages. Economics, health, communication, science, technology, social/family relations, art, education, transportation—in a glocal world, people are communicating across domains. I personally believe this will be the most logical place for the birth of a global church planting movement.

International Churches

International churches have been springing up for the past fifteen years in major cities around the world. Expatriates who go to live as a minority in a particular place find themselves worshiping with believers from every nation and in every domain. Rich and poor, diplomats and businesspeople, black and white, and representatives of every language — these people are perhaps in the biggest gold mines of church multiplication that we have in the world today. (But do they realize that?) They are the most connected churches of all because their membership represents every single domain of society.

Most act as havens for people who need to find a community of faith and catch their breath in nations that are not their home. However, of all churches in existence today, these churches could capture the potential of a global movement and be at the forefront. International community churches exist in almost every nation and could become the strategic hubs from which all else would flow.

Airports

Continental Airlines in Houston, Texas, became the target of flight attendants who started Bible studies, and from there studying the Bible spread to other airports. I emailed Andrew Jones once, talking about major cities that a global church planting movement would focus on. He emailed back saying it may not be cities as much as places in cities — airports in particular. I think it's a brilliant idea.

City Centers

Everything is in the city center, whereas most churches have been specialized and homogenized. The overarching homogeneous principle of global churches will be the city, and in those city centers, everything is possible. In New York City, Redeemer Church, where Tim Keller pastors, is an example, but so is Brooklyn Tabernacle and Times Square Church.

Cyberspace

I have no clue what this will look like, but it will be a reality. In the first Great Awakenings of America and England, evangelists went as far as the roads and the English language would take them. Today the roads are limitless because we travel anywhere we want to go with relative ease. The primary form of communication is the Internet. I believe the next awakening will be the final awakening because we are so connected globally with very little isolation in the cities. We had a Vietnamese exchange student live with us during high school and some of his college years. His dad and I email. His dad knows a little English, but on the Internet, he can translate and find the right words, and we communicate.

Multiethnic Churches

When my son started NYU, we visited Times Square Church together and I felt as though we were worshiping with the whole world. No one single race or nation dominated; it was everyone and everything—the closest thing to what heaven must be like that I've seen in terms of powerful worship and ethnic diversity. The church is involved in loads of humanitarian work, while at the same time being highly evangelistic. Seoul, Singapore, Lagos, Jakarta, and Hong Kong all have similar churches in the city centers. If I were planting today, that's where I'd want to be. These types of churches in America come closest to being potential players.

Global Destinations

Vacation and entertainment possibly could drive much of this communication. Places where people like to visit and different ethnicities could flatten the ability to connect. I recently spoke at the annual convention of the Race Track Chaplaincy of America. Who ever would have thought that churches were being planted on horse race tracks for all the people who work there? Most of them move from track to track, which means the opportunity to get a movement going is high. It's happening—and it was started thirty-five years ago not by a preacher but by a man named Sam Roberts, a layman and recovering alcoholic. Churches are now expanding internationally.

Not surprisingly, Ed Smith, the current president of the organization, is a businessman. He has plans to move forward with the idea into South America, Australia, Hong Kong, and other places. Pat Day, one of the top winning jockeys of all time, is their "ambassador" and is heavily involved in the ministry. He found Jesus after experiencing an incredibly downward-spiraling road. When he became a Christian, other well-intentioned Christians advised him to get out of the horse racing industry immediately. He was going to do exactly that until he realized that if he left, he would be taking his witness with him. So he stayed and became a remarkable influence in that realm for Christ.

What if there were churches in casinos? Why not? I think Jesus would like that. People need help there, too. It's exciting to me to see people from whatever area of the marketplace get involved.

Common Global Needs

People across nations are coming together to solve global problems, pooling their resources to tackle serious issues concerning the environment, health care, and the like. It could well be that churches will be planted as part of the solution.

What If?

Jews drove the first Jesus movement that seeded the gospel and engaged the entire world—all the way to the Gentiles. I believe the final Jesus movement (if it happens in the next two hundred years) will be seeded by the Muslims who will then take the gospel to the ends of the earth. Islam is not going away—and it will be a major religion of the future. Think about it. There are only two highly evangelistic religions in the world today—Islam and Christianity. What would be the impact if Muslims fanned their evangelistic fervor into faith in Jesus Christ?

Since we don't really know where the movement will come from, I have a proposal. What if faith communities in all of these flat places come together to strategically pray and seek God? That is more likely to bring it about than capitalizing on any single space because it will take all of them. It's crucial to understand that for a global church planting movement to take place, it will involve all of these places and all of these models. Those who insist theirs is the only way or even the primary way will be cut from the team. Multiethnic megachurches and Anglo house churches ... and everything in between ... will do it.

When this movement happens, it won't be tied to a single place or model but to Jesus and his church, period. Arrogance, egotism, and expertise will have no place in this movement. Prayer, faith, dependence, community, and openness will describe this movement above all else. Revelation 5:9–10 gives us a hint: "With your blood you purchased men for God from every tribe and language and people and nation. You have made them to be a kingdom and priests to serve our God, and they will reign on the earth."

Bringing It Home

Dick Bashta once said that the Great Commission will one day become the Great Completion. I believe there is no greater time to be alive than today and to see it happen. In a relay race, the two most important runners are the first and the last. The first one sets the pace for the other three runners. The two in between have to keep the pace. However, the last runner is the one who matters most—he has to bring it on home. He must not only keep the pace but must stay in front and catch the other runners; he must make up for what was lost and gain ground against those who are in front. Because I believe we, the next awakening, are the final awakening, I feel as though we are living in the final heat of the race. We must bring it on home.

Jesus answered: "Watch out that no one deceives you. For many will come in my name, claiming, 'I am the Christ,' and will deceive many. You will hear of wars and rumors of wars, but see to it that you are not alarmed. Such things must happen, but the end is still to come. Nation will rise against nation, and kingdom against kingdom. There will be famines and earthquakes in various places. All these are the beginning of birth pains.

"Then you will be handed over to be persecuted and put to death, and you will be hated by all nations because of me. At that time many will turn away from the faith and will betray and hate each other, and many false prophets will appear and deceive many people. Because of the increase of wickedness, the love of most will grow cold, but he who stands firm to the end will be saved. And this gospel of the kingdom will be preached in the whole world as a testimony to all nations, and then the end will come."

Matthew 24:4 – 14

The New Math

$MC^2 + FP = GC$

The missional church (MC), locally and globally (^{2}), when working in flat places (FP) produces glocal churches (GC). When we start a church, we are not just starting a church for that community. We are starting a church for the world, based out of that community. Every church you plant, you are planting for the billions of people who live on the earth. You are planting churches for the world.

PART 3

THE SUM TOTAL

Chapter 10

STARTING A CHURCH-STARTING CENTER IN YOUR CHURCH

L(r+a+t+c) + Systems + M(dna) = CPC

Once church leaders catch a vision for church multiplication, it spreads like wildfire. They soon find that it's not enough to plant one or two churches. These visionary leaders are beginning church-starting centers inside their churches that make church planting the very heartbeat of the church.

You will recall Brian Bloye's story about how his church began small, supporting church plants and eventually hiring a church planting intern to begin new churches. The rest of the story is that the members of West Ridge took another leap and started a church planting school in their church. The first year, fourteen church planters participated in the school. In 2007 they will plant at least eight churches. Here is their story.

> Blog posted by Brian Bloye
> Pastor, West Ridge Church, Dallas, Georgia
>
> I felt that God was leading us to start a school to train up and send out planters. We had no clue how to get it off the ground; we just knew we were supposed do to it. God hooked me up with Bob Roberts. I had heard that he had started a CP school at NorthWood, so I grabbed a moment with him at a conference in

Atlanta to pick his brain. From that meeting, I walked away with a fresh vision of what God wanted to do at West Ridge Church. We were going to be a church that started other churches, and God was going to raise up a school to accomplish it.

In 2005, I hired a guy from the Georgia Baptist Convention named Jim Akins. Jim had been a church planter and was currently working as a church planter strategist.

In August 2005, with a lot of help from Bob Roberts and the Glocalnet Team, we launched the West Ridge School of Church Planting. Our first class had 14 participants. Out of that class, CP teams developed and we launched four new churches here in the Atlanta area. As we trained these new planters over a nine-month period, God began to speak to families in our own congregation about leaving West Ridge to join these new churches. It was an amazing experience to commission these new churches and to watch them leave our school with several of our own families. Many of these were families that had been with us for many years and were involved in major roles of leadership.

In August 2006, with the start of a new class of planters, God gave me a vision to train up, send out, and plant 25 strong multiplying congregations in 25 counties within a 50-mile radius of our own church within three years. Since we're in a large metropolitan area, there are nearly 5 million people within 50 miles. The class of 2007, with 16 participants, will plant eight new churches here in the Atlanta area. As we network together with our daughter churches, we feel that within the 10 years we will be able to plant hundreds of churches, not just in Atlanta, but all over the world.

This vision has truly excited our church. At first our people were almost offended that I was challenging them to leave and go with a new church plant. Now it has become part of our culture. It's now part of our DNA. People at West Ridge know that at any minute God could call them to be part of a new work. It keeps things exciting and interesting. Now we don't simply judge our success on how many people God is bringing to West Ridge but on how many people He is sending out.

I dream of every church being a church planting center. One of the best things you can do is to begin to train church planters in your church. That suggestion may sound foreign to those who think some outside organization or denomination should do that. However, it ought to be the most natural thing in the world for the local church to do. It's the point at which a mature couple decides to start having children and begins raising them. The family values of presence and "being there" have a lot to do with the passing of DNA between the mother church and the daughter churches.

There was a period of time when we didn't require our planters to be part of our church; we just had them come to the classes we offered. That crew never did multiply like the rest who were part of our family. The multiplying gene didn't transfer, so we went back to having all the interns at NorthWood week in and week out to catch all of the nuances. We still allow them to visit other churches to learn, but we've learned there is something about presence and "being there" that helps the training sink in.

We began to develop a church-starting center when Brian Lightsey, a church planter from Austin, showed up and said he felt he wanted to be an intern. I was excited initially, but then it dawned on me: "What do I do with him?" It took some time to develop a game plan. We now have a manual and an entire process for our internship program and church planting center. It began to work so well that I received some funds for a period to grow our program from two interns per year to four. Then we lost our funding. I thought it was the worst thing that had ever happened. It wasn't.

I invited anyone who wanted to be a part to join our nine-month internship, as long as they went through a preassessment. At that point, we went from four to eight church planting interns—and this year we have fourteen. Addition—simply adding one more here and there—requires money and mimicking. Multiplication requires passion and creativity.

Planter Support

Vision360 has used the following chart in helping to get church planters on their feet. You can see some of the same basic steps to creating a church-starting center that I will describe below (see Figure 16).

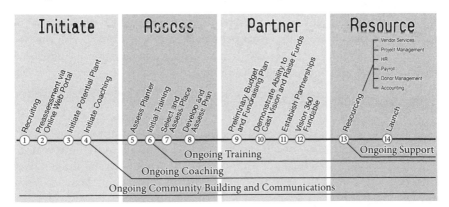

Figure 16: Vision360 Planter Support

1. Recruit

The first step to creating a church-starting center is to recruit. Recruiting may take place through natural streams such as colleges, seminaries, and even your own church members. The people you recruit have to feel wanted. Hang out where they hang out; get to know them. At first it takes time to recruit people to sign on to your vision. However, after a few successful plants, people will be knocking on your door to be a part of what's happening.

2. Assess

The next step is to assess your recruits. Vision360 has one of the best one-week assessment processes available at the Green Lakes Center in Wisconsin. Of course, less intense tools are available, such as online assessments and other self-assessing tools. These can tell you if the person you're considering is someone with whom you want to work. Though we are assessing for the point person in the plant, along the way we often find team members who won't be the planter but could function in other roles. Sometimes someone comes along who seems as if he or she will be the perfect point planter, but in time it becomes clear that this person would function better in a different role. This is why taking the time to assess is so crucial.

Assessments are of no value if you aren't willing to tell people honestly what you think and what the results say. I've heard people say that they would never tell someone they shouldn't plant a church if that's what they want to do. I passionately disagree with that thinking; it is irresponsible and insensitive not to be honest with someone. Despite having their emotional well-being and self-confidence at stake, not to mention the money, I now give it my best shot after having watched a couple of guys crash and burn. We fear that by telling someone "no" we are going to be the guy about whom the next Rick Warren or Mark Driscoll writes and says, "Bob Roberts told me I shouldn't plant, but I did and look how well it went."

Keep in mind that the odds of that happening aren't high. Sadly, there really aren't that many exceptional people. Better to be honest with the process and the person and be wrong than to ignore your misigivings and wind up with lots of people crashing and burning.

3. Train

Next you need to train and equip your recruits. Make no mistake about it — this is work. Every church that is going to train church planters needs a curriculum and systems to accomplish it. Teaching is giving information; training is helping your recruits learn to fulfill the various tasks they will need to master to be successful. Steve Addison, an exceptional church planting leader in Australia, says the best training is "in time" and "in teams."

He's right, and for that reason we never consider our training and teaching the final word.

The more model driven your training and teaching is, the more specific you will have to be. The more model oriented you are, the more your recruits have to learn to think, read, evaluate, and so on. We do have a "set menu" that we want all of our planters to understand, such as the theology of the kingdom. We also have various projects we want them to do. In addition, some will attend a Green House by Neil Cole, or a boot camp with ACTS 29, or a Purpose Driven conference with Ron Sylvia, or other things. It all has to do with what kind of model and church they are going to plant. Help them select their model based on their age, culture, generation, philosophy, and the like.

4. Coach

Creating a church-starting center requires ongoing coaching and mentoring. If you do this right, the majority of your time will be spent on the front end with your church planters. After that, they need to be accountable to their own prospectus that they have developed. Remember that your system and the building blocks of what you are trying to create are for the masses — not for the A+ players. They will do it with or without you.

I also believe that having multiple mentors who can provide coaching is essential. I've told our planters to make sure they keep a running list of what they want to learn from different people. For example, I have one person I look to for spiritual maturity. I turn to another person for issues related to management. I turn to someone else when I want to talk about issues dealing with growth.

Ironically, the best mentors for a church planter will often decline if asked. I never formally ask someone to mentor me. I just observe a particular skill or trait someone can teach me, and I ask them questions over lunch or dinner. When I've started mastering what they teach, I drop them a note and let them know my progress. That way, the next time I call, they feel as though our time together is profitable.

Intentional Training

> Suppose one of you wants to build a tower. Will he not first sit down and estimate the cost to see if he has enough money to complete it? For if he lays the foundation and is not able to finish it, everyone who sees it will ridicule him, saying, "This fellow began to build and was not able to finish."
>
> Luke 14:28–30

If you are going to create a church-starting center inside your local church, you must give potential church planters clear expectations. At NorthWood, we require our church planters to complete a prospectus. It is a several-page document that details their action plan and strategy, along with funding issues, that enables others to see what they are doing and allows others to contribute.

The second major item we require of planters is that they develop small groups. If they can't start a small group, how do they think they can start a church?

The third major project involves working in the inner city on a specific area of need.

The fourth major assignment is a global practicum. We take them to the country our church has adopted — Vietnam — and they get to see a different culture and learn how to engage and interact.

We also use two templates to train our planters over a nine-month period. One is how to start a church, which challenges church planters to process seven crucial steps. The rest of this chapter will discuss these seven steps or processors that a church can use as building blocks to develop its own curriculum or training program for church planters. The other is how to engage and start with society, which is our developmental domain practice.

There was a period in my life where I began to get confused about all I was learning. What to listen to, what to act on — it was very muddled, especially when people I respected a lot began to disagree. In reaction, I developed a grid through which I could understand all I was learning. I wanted to know how to process, plan, and develop — I needed a map to do all of that.

In the early 1990s I began to use the following seven processors, not just for myself but for other planters whom we were developing. The order in which you process them is important; how you address the first determines how you will answer the second and so on (see Figure 17).

Call ➔ Values ➔ Purpose ➔ Vision ➔ Strategy ➔ Leadership ➔ Evaluation

Figure 17: Seven Processors for Church Planters

Processor 1: Call

Everything starts with call. What has God called you to do? Sometimes our call can become confused with function, project, or action. That is merely the outgrowth of the inner voice that is calling us. I used to think that I was called to "preach," and then I discovered in reality that I was called to the kingdom and preaching was merely a function.

- Call is something unique to every person.
- Call requires certain preconditions, talents, abilities, and so on.
- Call reveals its presence by the enjoyment and sense of renewed energies its practice yields us.
- Call is something that must be searched for.[1]

How you interpret call is critical because it will determine what you give your life to for the long term. Call is a question of "who" you are listening to (God) and who you are becoming. The Latin word for "call" is *voca*, which means "voice." The German word *Beruf* denotes the idea of an inner voice, a spiritual call. James Hillman describes the poignancy of the call in *The Soul's Code*:

> There is more to a human life than our theories of it allow. Sooner or later something seems to call us onto a particular path. You may remember this something as a signal moment in childhood when an urge out of nowhere, a fascination, a peculiar turn of events struck like an annunciation: This is what I must do, this is what I've got to have. This is who I am.[2]

The priority of the call is essential. It's the reason we do what we do. It's the motivation for what we do. It is the standard of evaluation for what we do. It's the thing that separates us from the pack. Personal passion, a compelling sense of mystery, and an affirmation from others are all part of understanding one's call. Of course, God's Word, gifting, personality, understanding, and personal issues also come into play.

Processor 2: Values

Once we know our call, we begin to look at the values placed deep within us. All of our values are placed deep inside and determine who we are in a unique way. Do you know the four to six values that you practice without thinking?

Most of us could make a list of fifty or sixty values we could hope to possess. We get them from the Bible, culture, families, and other places. However, four to six values drive your life without your even being consciously aware of them. These core values are like a matrix through which you process everything. There are five ways to discover such values:

a. Study significant events in your life.
b. Look for patterns.
c. Identify what your successes and failures have in common.
d. Examine your deep hurts.
e. Let others who know you well help you discover them.

Nothing is as critical to a church planter as knowing and understanding values, especially personal values. You can do without a good purpose statement—even without a tightly mapped out strategy. However, value misalignment will kill you.

I've seen it happen. A new pastor says he is pastor at First Church Heaven, and it "couldn't be better." The people refer to their pastor as St. Ed and say "he couldn't be better." Six months later, you see the guy and he says it has become First Church Hell. The church members believe the pastor is now demon-possessed and definitely not a Christian! What happened? Are they that good or that bad? Probably not. What has happened is that both parties see values in conflict that were never in sync from the start. My definition of a *value* is: *a conviction regarding truth that determines behavior.*

Values are not just beliefs. We say we believe things, but they don't determine our behavior. We say we value marriage, yet we have the highest divorce rates in the world. Why? We may believe in the value of marriage intellectually, but not in practice and not in behavior. Values determine behavior and are the hooks on which everything else is hung. They may be good or bad, but they don't change; they are fairly consistent. You don't change your values; you are your values. You can't adopt someone else's values because they're not who you are.

Values are also not practices. You may say you value small groups. However, small groups are merely the means of the real value: community of discipleship. A small group is the delivery system of that specific value.

Without values, there will be no direction. Arnold Toynbee in the 1940s studied twenty-one leading civilizations of the world. He found that most civilizations didn't fall from being overtaken, but instead from experiencing a "schism of the soul," something he even foresaw for the West.

He said that this schism started with a fall into a sense of abandon. Escapism. Not dealing with problems. Drift. Guilt. Promiscuity of life. Values are the foundations on which we build life. The Bible has this to say about values:

> By the grace God has given me, I laid a foundation as an expert builder, and someone else is building on it. But each one should be careful how he builds. For no one can lay any foundation other than the one already laid, which is Jesus Christ. If any man builds on this foundation using gold, silver, costly stones, wood, hay or straw, his work will be shown for what it is, because the Day will bring it to light. It will be revealed with fire, and the fire will test the quality of each man's work. If what he has built survives, he will receive his reward. If it is burned up, he will suffer loss; he himself will be saved, but only as one escaping through the flames.
>
> 1 Corinthians 3:10–15

Values are critical to the church planter because the values come from the planter to the church. He establishes the values of the new church without even trying. Who the planter is determines the culture of the entire plant. That means that the planter determines overall the behavior, character, focus, goals, norms, and even priorities. All of these can be predicted from an understanding of someone's values.

Processor 3: Purpose

The call and values are "who" questions; now the "what" question comes into play. What am I here for? What am I to do? What are we as a church, a ministry, or a group to do? Call answers the question, "Who is going to direct my life?" Values answer the question, "Who does God want me to be?" Purpose answers the question, "What does God want me to do?"

I learned about purpose from two pastors, Rick Warren and Myles Munroe. It was the single most significant thing I had to learn about starting a church—but beyond that it was also a key lesson about life. No wonder Rick Warren's book *The Purpose Driven Life* has sold as it has—people are hungry for purpose. Author Myles Munroe says that without knowing and understanding your purpose, you can never be fulfilled in life because "purpose is the master motivation and the mother of commitment."[3] In his book *In Pursuit of Purpose*, he makes the following observations:

- Purpose precedes production.
- Purpose is constant—plans may change, not purpose.
- Purpose is the master of motivation.
- Purpose is the mother of commitment.
- Purpose is seen in the nature of a thing.

Purpose is discovered not from the thing but from the creator. The nature of something is a powerful clue to its purpose and potential. God is a God of purpose.[4] The questions, *Who am I? Why am I here? Where did I come from? What was I born to do? Where am I going?* all relate to purpose.

Substitutions for knowing our purpose lead to futility. Busyness keeps us from even thinking about it. Envy makes us devalue and neglect it. Ignorance and failure to reflect and examine keep us confused about it. Other people may have a purpose in mind for our lives, but other people's plans are no substitute for discovering God's purpose.

God has a purpose for all of us, and we must know what it is if we are to accomplish his plan for our lives and churches. Proverbs 20:5 tells us, "The purposes of a man's heart are deep waters, but a man of understanding draws them out." Proverbs 19:21 shows us that God's purpose outweighs our plans: "Many are the plans in a man's heart, but it is the LORD's purpose that prevails."

Once you think you have discovered your purpose in life, there are four tests to confirm it. (1) You can ask yourself, "Is this from God?"—and you know it is. (2) You must make sure that it somehow embodies the Great Commission that Jesus gave us. (3) You must avoid making it complicated. Make sure your purpose, as you understand it, is simple and focused. (4) Finally, is it clear enough to give direction, strategy, and a plan of action? I love what God has to say about his purposes:

> Remember the former things, those of long ago;
>> I am God, and there is no other;
>> I am God, and there is none like me.
> I make known the end from the beginning,
>> from ancient times, what is still to come.
> I say: My purpose will stand,
>> and I will do all that I please.
> From the east I summon a bird of prey;
>> from a far-off land, a man to fulfill my purpose.
> What I have said, that will I bring about;
>> what I have planned, that will I do.
>
> Isaiah 46:9–11

Processor 4: Vision

Once we know our call, values, and purpose, we must decide the particular need we feel called to fulfill. This need is specific and fits within the constraints of time and place. "Where there is no revelation, the people cast off restraint; but blessed is he who keeps the law" (Proverbs 29:18).

Vision is the practical fulfillment in a specific way of your purpose. It's what you see; it's where you are going. It is God revealing himself to you. There is a sense of intuition at work in all of this. Research has shown that visionary leaders possess more than usual intuition. Intuition is the result of bringing together knowledge and experience.[5] Two things make us move from where we are: (1) the discovery of a better way; or (2) frustration with the way things are.

Vision helps us move to that next place. You can be sure that whatever vision we see involves risk. However, despite the risk, our vision is so compelling that it causes us to move to the other side. Vision is always a future paradise; there is no trash on the beach. It is vision that creates the future shore of what we long to be a part of.

However, vision is not just a hazy dream; it is specific. It encapsulates everything God has called us to do. It doesn't take power and position to enact one's vision. God can use a common shepherd and all of his experiences to help him achieve success. Psalm 78:70–72 says, "He chose David his servant and took him from the sheep pens; from tending the sheep he brought him to be the shepherd of his people Jacob, of Israel his inheritance. And David shepherded them with integrity of heart; with skillful hands he led them."

Sometimes we get discouraged in our vision. The things that sink our ships are impatience, lack of resources, complacency, small thinking, monsters that never appear, fatigue, depression, and old thinking. We must constantly keep our vision afloat despite these obstacles.

God gave me this passage from Habakkuk on my twelfth anniversary at NorthWood. "Then the LORD replied: 'Write down the revelation and make it plain on tablets so that a herald may run with it. For the revelation awaits an appointed time; it speaks of the end and will not prove false. Though it linger, wait for it; it will certainly come and will not delay'" (Habakkuk 2:2–3). Afterward, I wrote about vision in my journal: "Over the years I ran because of vision. Passion was my fuel. Enthusiasm my commodity. Discouragement my ever-present enemy who had to be fought. Joy is the result of achievement. Depression, the result of failure. But behind it all—God. Thy Kingdom come; thy will be done. Now!"

Make sure you aren't the only one with vision. Aubrey Malphurs teaches that it isn't enough for one person to have vision.[6] Naturally, there must be a point person, but there must be other vision casters as well. He classifies them as casters, clarifiers, and communicators. George Barna writes, "In successful churches, people were encouraged to articulate the vision through lifestyle, not just the repetition of right words. Behavioral modeling was the most effective means of communication."[7] I also like what Barna says about the viral nature of vision: "Vision has no force, power or impact unless it spreads."[8]

Processor 5: Strategy

Strategy is the action plan. It's where one's call, values, purpose, and vision all merge. Good strategies start by pinpointing where you are going and what it will take to get there. It's important to be able to paint a picture of where you're headed and to set goals or milestones that should happen along the way. Goals determine action steps. When placed in the context of a timeline, budget, and process, you have your strategy.

Strategies should detail:

- whom you are going to reach
- how you are going to reach them
- what you will use as your action plan

You will also want to identify in your strategy the costs and a rough timeline of your milestones. Setting goals like these gives you something to measure and focus your efforts. There are a thousand different strategies for a thousand different churches; each one is unique. Just consider how many different ways you could accomplish goals related to a new church plant. However, here is a short list to get you started strategizing. Decide your strategies for:

- community development
- core groups
- small groups
- T-Life (discipleship)
- funding
- worship (e.g., launching your first service)

Processor 6: Leadership

"The things you have heard me say in the presence of many witnesses entrust to reliable men who will also be qualified to teach others" (2 Timothy 2:2). The most important action step after determining a strategy is identifying who is going to do it. This is where leadership and delegation come into play. As long as your ministry is growing, you will be raising up leaders. Chances are high that your ministry is growing *because* you are raising up leaders. The job description of anyone in the ministry can be defined by two words—leadership development.

A new church plant will grow only to the level and quality of leaders who are raised up and engaged. A few months after I started NorthWood, I began to meet with a group of men to disciple them. My goal was to help them get on their feet spiritually; I actually didn't do it to raise up leaders. However, every one of these men became a key leader in our church. Today I still meet with a group of men. Many of these men are already leaders, and some will become even more significant leaders.

In a new church, start with turning outsiders into insiders. Do this as quickly as possible as people come on board. They have to feel as though they are part of something larger than the Sunday event.

The next step is to turn converts into disciples, through what I've described as creating a culture for transformation that changes people's behavior, not merely passes along information.

The final step is turning disciples into ministers. This is where you practice mobilization through spiritual gifts. Identify the reliable men and women in your church and their giftings. Entrust responsibilities to them and educate them through mentoring so that they can emulate what they have seen you do.

Another function of leadership is determining how the church is organized and how it makes decisions. Whatever polity you use, keep it simple and make sure accountability is built into the system. Make it clear to those on your team how it works.

Processor 7: Evaluation

As leaders, we must constantly evaluate ourselves, our ministry, and our church. As you demonstrate your willingness to critique yourself, others will be more open to change in the ministry and in themselves. If they see you as personally resistant or inflexible regarding feedback, good luck.

Each year, I send out a personal evaluation form to fifty new members — men and women, youth and adults. On it, they are invited to critique everything from my character and leadership style to the church programs. It isn't always fun to get those responses back! Yet this evaluation has served as a base for things that need to change and improve.[9]

When I spoke about this topic at a seminary one day, a pastor later told me that I was doing something dangerous. In his mind, this process could open up a can of worms, and I agree that there is some truth to what he was saying. At the same time, I cannot discount the benefits of knowing versus guessing how I'm doing. I told him, "The only difference between you and me is this: I know what the people I work with are thinking and you don't."

I've found that it doesn't hurt a healthy leadership to critique itself. If anything, most people are impressed with the idea and welcome it. However, if you choose to open yourself up to evaluation, expect to encounter areas that need improvement. Church growth can be defined in two words: problem solving.

Here are some tips I've learned over the years about the role of evaluation and leadership:

- Act according to your purpose.
- Evaluate what you are doing and how it is working.
- Learn to be a diagnostician.
- Be flexible.
- Realize you can't keep everybody happy.
- Raise up leaders constantly.
- Focus on infrastructure.
- Let your faith put you out on a limb — always risk.

The joy of victory is proportionate to the amount of risk involved. Risk puts us at God's disposal and keeps our faith vibrant.

> "Come to the edge," he said.
> They said, "We are afraid."
> "Come to the edge," he said.
> They came.
> He pushed them ... And they flew!
> Guillaume Apollinare[10]

The New Math

L (r + a + t + c) + Systems + M(dna) = CPC

The location (L) of your center is important. Training needs to take place in local churches if the desired result is multiplication. You will want to recruit (r), assess (a), train (t) and coach (c) church planters. Systems must in place so that the DNA of the mother (M) is passed on. The result is a church planting center (CPC).

Chapter 11

MORE THAN JUST NUMBERS

M + E + P > $

When Nikki and I moved to northeast Tarrant County to start North-Wood, I didn't know what to expect financially. Hedging my bets, I had just secured a job as a night stocker at a local Kroger store before I came. However, I didn't have to take that additional job because of the growth of our new church and the offerings that came in weekly.

I had been told to be extremely careful when discussing money. The advice was not to harp on it. In a time when many pastors of huge ministries were living extravagant lifestyles with many possessions, I didn't want to come across as one of them.

The message I often heard was that God will provide if you just have faith—but for God's sake don't talk about money or you'll run off the very people you're trying to reach!

Candidly, we nearly went broke following that line of thinking. I remember we were about six years into the ministry and struggling financially. I was tired of the constant stress over money. I heard Bill Hybels once tell about his early days at Willow Creek. After six years, something had to give, so he began to talk about money and finances. That revelation shocked me—I never would have thought he would have to do that. It made me reexamine my view of money and finances, and I'm glad I did.

There is no greater stress point in a new church than that of finances. Church planters often have to face the reality that there may not be enough offering to cover their salary. A new church can decide or a denominational committee can set what a salary should be, but the actual paycheck is sometimes very different. That's why the first figure in my formula for handling money in new church plants is (M)—miracles.

I love to be around church planters and hear their stories of how God has blessed them unexpectedly—there are so many miracle stories. Land is donated; budgets are provided for; an asset is made available just in the nick of time.

I learned this firsthand. After I heard Hybels tell about his experience, I decided to talk to our church about money. I began by dealing with how consumerism had turned us into greedy people and how we could never be content if we were driven by the newer and nicer. The response was fantastic, and I immediately realized that not talking about money was a big mistake—not just in terms of the needs of the church, but in terms of people being free financially.

Phone Call to New York

We had always dreamed of a lot of land. Our mother church had given us eleven acres. However, a creek ran through it, and it was going to cost a couple of million dollars to reclaim it. Our location was okay but not great.

In 1986 a small group of church planters from Texas traveled to Southern California, where we met Bob Logan, Thom Wolf, and Rick Warren. We had previously been told that at our growth rate, if we didn't hurry up and build, our growth would slow down. However, all three of these men cautioned us not to be in a hurry because of the piece of land we had.

When we traveled to Southern California, they were already clearing off our acreage. As I listened to the other men speak, I knew they were right. But I didn't know what to do since we had been given the land. I had seen another piece of land, seventy-five acres strong, but a developer from a bank in New York had the land and was getting ready to build on it.

One day I called the banker in New York—we Texans will do anything. I told him, "We have eleven acres with a beautiful creek that runs through the property. Why don't I make you a deal? We'll give you our eleven acres for four of your corner acreage. He laughed and said incredulously, "You Texas preachers—you guys blow me away! You think I would do that?"

"Sir, I just wanted to give you the first chance!" He let me know he wasn't interested.

No Stopping Us Now

I've since learned to take what you've got, and that's what I did here. We began to build on our land. A few years later, we were five years old and looking at building our second worship center because of our growth. We heard that because of some shady land deals, a good portion of the land along a major road in our area was in foreclosure. It was the very piece of land that the banker had, and he had never built on it. A piece of land that had been sold for millions, we were able to purchase for half a million dollars.

We had to sell our existing building, move to a shopping center, and wait to raise money to build on our land—a process that took several years instead of two as we had planned. But as I wrote in my earlier book *Transformation*, that too was from God. God was about to teach some incredible lessons in faith and the real purpose for the church beyond our four walls.

Finally, we were able to build, and we continued to grow. As I write this, we are building a 2,000-seat auditorium and can't wait to enter it. However, we would have liked to build a 3,500-seat auditorium. And we could have—if we had dramatically stopped all the church planting, inner-city work, and global work that we are doing.

One of the parties helping with our building committee even suggested as much; I didn't have to say a word. Our committee explained to the man how that would not be consistent with who we are. We have some big dreams about how we want to engage society and the world, and we are not stopping now. In fact, something significant happened—natural gas was found on our land and we recently signed a contract. My point is that God provides what you need just at the time you need it.

Calculating by Faith

We have always tried to plan our budgets and buildings carefully, and to do so in advance so that our people can give regularly. This is particularly important for new churches (especially with new believers) because it takes time for the people to begin the discipline of giving. However, God has been teaching me that when budgets are too planned, we don't teach faith as we should. Sometimes we have to learn to give in faith even when we don't have all the answers.

It is crucial for planters (and pastors as well) to learn to give throughout their walk. Initially, planters give even though they're broke because they know they are going to have to model giving for the rest of the church. I believe the pastor should be the most generous person in the church. That doesn't mean that he gives the biggest amount, but perhaps he makes the largest sacrifice.

On at least one occasion, God impressed Nikki and me to clean out our savings. I had just made a long-term commitment to NorthWood in my heart, and things weren't easy at that time. I had also turned down a large church with a large salary. Nikki had told me I didn't even need to consider it. I agreed and told her, "Well, no big deal—all it would mean is preaching to more people and living in a bigger house. We're happy now."

In an unusual set of circumstances a few weeks later, we found ourselves moving to another, better house on our same salary at an incredible deal. God was teaching me that he is my provider!

God has used NorthWood and me to raise millions of dollars and to use those funds to bring glory to him and to produce fruit for his kingdom. I don't always have the money myself, but because of connections or opportunities that he has allowed, I get to be a channel.

Recently, when we were raising money for the new facility, I was praying about what God wanted Nikki and me to give. We wanted to give our biggest gift ever and one of the largest in the church. My first two books were coming out and I made a pledge based on the best possible sales scenario. Though they've done okay, as usual, it wasn't as much as I dreamed it could have been.

Amazingly, Nikki and I were able to keep our pledge. Whether it was a speaking gift or something else, we kept up with it. Then something out of the blue happened that allowed us to pay our pledge in full—and some six months before it was due. We've now been able to give more to God in the first three months of this year than we have in any single year of our giving—and we have kids in private universities! God is good. I'm not saying that only giving money to build buildings matters; some of the most exciting giving I've done has been to help the poor and to support other projects. But if a church is going to engage its community and uses "size" to make a huge impact, then you have phenomenal opportunity.

Here's what God taught me. I had faith to make a pledge because I saw a scenario in which that size gift could be possible. I more than fulfilled the pledge, but it wasn't in the way I originally saw God doing it. I realized even my faith was too calculating. What would have happened had I trusted God for twice that amount?

Educating Others about Money

It's an unusual feeling listening to businesspeople talk about what their next million-dollar gift will be. As I listened to one particular conversation, I began to talk to God about my own giving: "God, I'm no millionaire by a long shot, but I'd love to give a million to you in a single gift." As I wondered what it must be like, not just to have money like them but to be able to give as they do, I said, "I'd give anything to be able to give a million bucks."

I even felt a lump in my throat and a certain sadness knowing that unless God worked a miracle, that was something I would never be able to accomplish. I think they could see the disappointment in my face and replied, "We'd like to be able to do what *you* do—connecting people and changing the world."

I realized that God wouldn't love me any more if I gave a million dollars. These guys do it for the same reason given by George Malone when asked why he climbed Mt. Everest—"Because I can." We may not be able to control all we give, but we should be giving as much as we can, which is the background of stewardship education.

As part of setting our stewardship education in motion, the first thing I did was to preach on it on a regular basis. In the early days of our church when I first began to teach about stewardship, I developed a sermon series about money matters (though not explicitly about giving and tithing). I had to start where they were. I recently completed a series called "Enuff!" on being content where you are and giving to the Lord. Our attendance hasn't decreased in response to this teaching. At times, if we position the series properly, giving actually goes up.

Second, we began to teach the Crown Financial Freedom course from Crown Financial Ministries, a program that helped us dramatically. Every time one of our groups goes through Crown, our giving always increases. The twelve-week course doesn't deal with giving that much; it deals more with the broader base of money management and teaches participants to develop a budget, track their spending, and so on. We encourage all of our planters to be certified in Crown Financial Freedom.

Third, we wrote stewardship lessons for our small group leaders to teach.

Fourth, we created a culture of giving by celebrating great things that happened as a result of giving, such as the stories I have just shared. In this way, we tied vision to giving. We began to have people share what was happening in their lives in relation to giving.

Fifth, we created a culture of giving by making sure that people in leadership roles were all tithing, at a minimum. We didn't want people determining the future of our church who weren't giving.

It's Not about the Money

The difficult financial struggles planters go through are essential to teaching them faith, dependence, and the sufficiency of God. These struggles are also crucial because a church has to decide if it's going to give. In the midst of dreaming great dreams about serving and helping people, a church will be limited in what it can do if people don't give.

Bottom line, it's really not about money. Rather, it's about faith, discipleship, growth, vision, and most important, scale—how big is your vision? There will be a relationship between vision and impact that only faith can develop.

Paul dealt with the same issues. Such issues aren't new, and they will never be (nor should it ever be) completely fixed. It's part of the discipleship process of faith and trust:

There is no need for me to write to you about this service to the saints. For I know your eagerness to help, and I have been boasting about it to the Macedonians, telling them that since last year you in Achaia were ready to give; and your enthusiasm has stirred most of them to action. But I am sending the brothers in order that our boasting about you in this matter should not prove hollow, but that you may be ready, as I said you would be. For if any Macedonians come with me and find you unprepared, we — not to say anything about you — would be ashamed of having been so confident. So I thought it necessary to urge the brothers to visit you in advance and finish the arrangements for the generous gift you had promised. Then it will be ready as a generous gift, not as one grudgingly given.

2 Corinthians 9:1 – 5

Why People Give

Kennon Callahan has written two outstanding books that deal with giving.[1] In them, he makes an effective argument for understanding the "why" behind people's giving patterns and principles. He establishes a fourfold premise for giving:

- It is part of discipleship.
- It is an act of worship.
- It is an expression of gratitude.
- It is a statement about what we believe and how seriously we believe it.[2]

He explains that people most often give to winning causes, and they want to be generous to what they perceive as a winning cause. He also explains how important the "asker" is — a youth in the church will solicit a different response from people than will the senior pastor.

Callahan also identifies five motivations for giving.[3] It's helpful to process which ones you most often use to motivate others and to understand that giving is different for every person in your church:

- compassion
- community
- challenge
- reasonableness
- commitment

Each Budget Is Unique

Where did the early church give its money? We know they gave to the poor. Establishing a pattern for giving to the poor and missions is critical; such a pattern should be built into the budget from day one. I feel sorry for some new churches; their denomination gives with one hand and takes with the other. The denomination may give them $2,000 per month, but then require two-thirds of that same money per month in what are often administrative expenses.

We know the early church gave to some of the leaders, and we also know that as the house meetings grew, so did the houses themselves. Peter's house was enlarged to handle the crowds, as were the houses of a number of wealthy Christians. I always assumed that house churches were eight to ten people—that is doubtful. Given the crowding in the cities, they could be as large as 50 or 150.

In Jakarta I visited with a godly man in his home in which he built a room for his own "house church," which handles 150 people! I've also visited with some house church pastors who have 75 to 150 in their house churches today. I think there is a reason most American churches average 75 people. And it's not because they're necessarily unhealthy; it just may be a sociological result of the way people gather.

The point is that each budget is going to be unique to the plant in size and scope. Each budgeting system has to change and grow as the new plant does. Starting a church as a congregation from day one is different and has different requirements than starting a house church. One is not better than the other; you just have to determine what God is calling you to do, given your particular skill set.

For example, I've encouraged one of our planters, a gymnast, to pursue his dream to go to Vegas and get a job with Cirque du Soleil. What better way to meet people who need Jesus and then serve them? He's looking at doing some "third space" gatherings as well. What he envisions may look more like a network of house churches, and that can alter how that type of church is funded. A particular approach will determine salaries, meeting places, utilities, administrative costs, and ministry costs. Let the people in those given areas help develop what their budget will look like.

Handling the Funds

How a planter collects, counts, reports, and manages the money and resources in the church will determine the level of confidence and willingness to give among the people.

This may sound basic, but you should collect the money during an offertory and take it to a private place to be counted. Don't have the same two people counting together all the time, but rotate the two people who are together. I encourage pastors not to be on the check-signing list in order to rule out the possibility of having their integrity questioned or challenged in this area.

Raising the Funds for a New Church

Raising funds starts with a group of individuals who feel called to help the planter. The prospectus I mentioned in the previous chapter becomes an important tool of communicating who you are and what you want to accomplish.

Raising funds from other churches is a key way to launch a new church. One of the key lessons we learned was that most planters had natural ties to several churches. If a planter walks up to a senior pastor at a church and asks for a quarter million dollars, chances are high that it isn't going to happen. However, if that planter requests help for eighteen to thirty-six months and wants only $300 to $1,000 a month from each sponsor church, he has a far greater chance of raising the money. If planters can do that with ten churches, their salary is usually covered at a minimum. Each church is also tied to a network or denomination, which represent further potential avenues for funding.

God Comes Through

I've come to believe that money is one of the chief discipleship factors—not just for a follower of Jesus, but also for a church. How we handle money and what we do with it will determine much of the future of a church. If you learn to trust God financially, you can trust him in many other ways as well. God always comes through when we do, and he often does so with more than what we need.

The New Math

$$M + E + P > \$$$

God is going to work miracles (M) as you start multiplying the church. If a church plant makes it, it will be a miracle; that's just part of God teaching you early on to trust him. Yet, we must also educate (E) and plan (P) regarding decisions involving money. If we do that, we will have more (>) than enough money ($) to do what God calls us to do.

Chapter 12

LIVING AS A MISSIONAL FAMILY

P + S + C = S

I remember the day Nikki and I got married. We were both scared, very stubborn, very independent, and about to join our lives together. The first year of our marriage was so bad that if we could have gotten out of it gracefully, we would have. I learned that people never really say "I do" at the altar—that's too easy. "I do" comes later on, when they want to quit but refuse to give up.

Because I was going into the ministry, I didn't feel like we could talk with anyone about what was going on because I was a "preacher" and "preachers don't have problems." What if someone knew I wasn't perfect? What if I was having problems in my marriage; was it all over? As seminary students, Nikki and I went to Sagamore Hill Baptist Church in Fort Worth. The pastor's wife had a Sunday school class for seminary students. We could go there and act as if we had no problems. But we intently listened to other couples talk about their problems so we could learn. It was fantastic!

We rocked on, and things would get better, then worse, then better. One day, we had a bad argument. We were yelling and blaming each other—you know, all the things that are going to fix a marriage! I was so angry I shot out of the house. As I drove around, it hit me. I had three choices. One was to divorce her; but if I did, I'd have to start over with someone else. And besides, I truly did love her; that was never in question.

Another option was to stay miserable the rest of my life—I didn't want that.

The third option was to fix it, and so we began to work on it—and we have ever since. I can honestly say that since that time, our marriage has improved every year.

One of the biggest challenges for any disciple, especially a church planter, is family life. Church leaders who are interested in practicing church multiplication must understand what a church planter will face. Missional families don't come easily.

What makes church planting so hard sometimes is that we're not just learning to plant a church; we're learning to do life. In the middle of trying to plant a new church, we're learning to become good husbands and fathers, wives and mothers, neighbors, even good Christians. Compounding that challenge is the fact that we're trying to learn all this stuff while we are up in front of everybody else telling them how to live. If a church planter's spouse isn't a part of the process, chances are the planter won't make it.

There are two key reasons why new churches fail. First, the leadership of the planter is not sufficient. Second, the marriage of the planter is not secure.

Not Enough Hours in the Day

As a planter, I've found there aren't enough hours in the day. I used to believe the key was balance. If I could just get a little more organized, that would change everything. It helped, but it didn't change everything.

I used to believe if our church could only get a little bigger, that would be the key. There would be more money for more staff and more help to alleviate some of my headaches. Once again, it helped, but it didn't do away with the stress. The more I organized, the more I could do. The more we grew, the more I had to reorganize; it was an ongoing cycle. I was always looking for that "elusive" item or area that, if I could only fix it, I would be balanced and life would be calm.

I love reading biographies, and I've come to realize that John Wesley, Winston Churchill, Abraham Lincoln, and the apostle Paul all had the same twenty-four hours. Their life was anything but balanced. Most great things we do are not because all the gauges are steady and the plane is flying level. If anything, we do great things while life is very much out of balance. There is nothing balanced about a father or mother going off to serve in a war. The key is to know where you live and to live in that moment completely. Most people fail because they attempt to keep in mind everything else that is going on, so they never focus on anything. When you're there, be there. Instead of striving for balance, live by priorities and goals.

I have learned many things. First, *there is enough time in the day to do everything you need to do*, but those things won't be done without sacrifice and unbalance. That is, if you really want to change the world, it requires discipline, not just meandering through life. Most of us want to change the world; we just want to do it in an easy or organized 1-2-3 sort of way. No one ever did that—not even Bible heroes.

Second, *give time to what really matters.* Your walk with God really matters — so I began to give him an hour a day as I began my day. At first I didn't have time, but I soon realized that if you want to change the world, you have to be on your face before God to hear what he's saying and condition yourself to recognize what he's doing during the day.

Also, I had read that a typical dad gives his kids only two minutes of undivided attention a day. On his deathbed, evangelist Billy Sunday said, "The world I've won, but my son I've lost." His son died an alcoholic.

Most preachers and their spouses take one of two extreme views of their kids. One is to feel sorry for them because everyone is looking at them. The other is to drive them hard because they're the "preacher's kids." Both are wrong. I committed to giving Ben and Jill two hours a day, two evenings a week, and all day Saturday. Something really cool happened. Not only did I give them time, I enjoyed them; to this day when they're in town or around, we get together and have a lot of fun. I've also taken them with me on trips around the world and brought them with me when I've met with significant people.

Nikki and I taught them how to act in public and practice protocol. I have no hesitation taking either one of them into the Oval Office with me. They know how to handle themselves — in public (though in private, well, someday I'll write a book on Jill).

Then I had to learn how to organize our church by its purpose. I began focusing on the goals for each year and developing an action plan with a budget, timeline, and so on. As NorthWood grew and as the ministry outside NorthWood also grew, the plan constantly called for realignment and more adjustment. Being a leader is stressful at times — there's just no getting around it. However, once again, most people who are changing the world don't do it kicking back. There is enough time to do everything you need to do, but you have to be organized and focused.

I also had to learn to exercise. I run forty-five minutes to an hour at least five days a week. It helps me handle stress and keeps my mind clear. When I'm running, I constantly come up with new solutions and new ideas.

Third, *I must live my life recognizing what God is doing and staying up to speed when unique opportunities come along.* If the other things aren't in place, there is no way I can do this. For me at least, this has been the key to why I've been able to be involved in so many things.

Handling Life's Stresses

A few years ago, I was examining my life and at the same time trying to help a young church planter with his. I came up with a metaphor for dealing with some of the stress in life (see Figure 18).

Figure 18: Starting Out as a Church Planter

We as church planters are like a kettle filled with water. That water is the water of life, and in that water is hope. Jesus described it this way: "Whoever believes in me, as the Scripture has said, streams of living water will flow from within him" (John 7:38).

When that water is first poured into us, everything is calm and not too difficult. We know we are supposed to give the water to others as instructed in Mark 9:41: "I tell you the truth, anyone who gives you a cup of water in my name because you belong to Christ will certainly not lose his reward." Thankfully, as our ministries grow, God ensures that much of our personal growth is taking place at the same time, lest we collapse under the weight of the burdens. Some of the stresses we can control; some are beyond our ability—yet we can all live in such a way as not to be destroyed by them.

Soon, however, things begin to heat up because of the growth of our ministry and life. We begin to realize that we are wrong about the idea that things are calm when we serve God. We imagine that when churches begin to grow, everything will be organized and orderly. So when things get hectic, we don't understand why. Growth then creates pressures that act as logs on the fire. That calm, cool water now starts to heat up (see Figure 19).

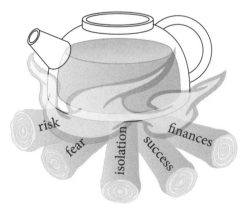

Figure 19: Church Planter Stress

"Logs" like risk and fear are usually the first to heat up the kettle. Having to live with the uncertainty of what you have done produces fears. Was this the greatest decision of your life or the worst? Some days the answer is unclear. Is this really going to work or not? Sometimes, it's not certain. Isolation, financial burdens, and even one's own "success" can produce stress in the new church, and the church planter's family begins to heat up as well.

Figure 20: Dangers Common to All Church Planters

Certain sediments are common to all church planters (see Figure 20). When the water starts to boil, the heat loosens those sediments and they poison our water. We begin to hurt others instead of being a blessing. Stress will bring out the deepest layers of our sediments, which can be summarized in three categories: character flaws, spiritual immaturity, and past hurts. Failure to deal with our junk leads to bitterness, blaming, addictions, and other forms of extreme behavior. These are the "all kinds of trials" Peter talks about that undergo the Refiner's fire:

> Praise be to the God and Father of our Lord Jesus Christ! In his great mercy he has given us new birth into a living hope through the resurrection of Jesus Christ from the dead, and into an inheritance that can never perish, spoil or fade—kept in heaven for you, who through faith are shielded by God's power until the coming of the salvation that is ready to be revealed in the last time. In this you greatly rejoice, though now for a little while you may have had to suffer grief in all kinds of trials. These have come so that your faith—of greater worth than gold, which perishes even though refined by fire—may be proved genuine and may result in praise, glory and honor when Jesus Christ is revealed. Though you have not seen him, you love him; and even though you do not see him now, you believe in him and are filled with an inexpressible and glorious joy, for you are receiving the goal of your faith, the salvation of your souls.
>
> 1 Peter 1:3–9

Character Flaws

There are no perfect people. Small, unaddressed weaknesses will continue to grow like a weed intent on destroying a plant. As John Maxwell has often said, "You are not as good as they say or as bad as they say." Spiritual maturity and wisdom are generally built through pain. Often, pastors or planters will equate their character and integrity with the growth of their ministry. This isn't good. Growing an organization is not necessarily equivalent with being a person of integrity. We have seen that.

Furthermore, as an organization grows, so does the exposure. If we aren't careful, those things can actually pollute us. Stress is an incredible opportunity for us to grow if only we will recognize it as such. We are shaped by values born out of situations in which we must choose right in spite of difficult circumstances.

Character is seen in two ways in the life of a planter. One is integrity — who the person is. The other is the courage to deal with headaches. Confrontation isn't fun; yet no church, ministry, or organization will go beyond the leader's ability not only to cast vision, but to keep the vision on track. The leader must be willing at times to lose in the short term for the sake of the long term.

Spiritual Immaturity

If our ministry is growing, we often equate that development with our spiritual maturity. It's not the same thing. A truer statement is that as our ministry grows, our maturity also must increase. Spiritual maturity comes from deep reflection and meditation on God's Word. It is never static; it is always moving in one direction or the other. Spiritual maturity is dependent on our ability to sit still and listen. How is your faith growing? What new things are you learning from God's Word? What is God teaching you?

Books and seminars are great, but nothing can replace your personal and specific instruction from God. Don't allow your sermon preparation to take the place of your personal spiritual preparation. Don't allow your religious work to be a substitute for your personal walk with God.

Past Hurts

No one gets a free pass in life. All of us have been hurt by someone deeply, and we have hurt someone deeply. How we handle those hurts affects how we learn to handle life. When we are in our twenties, we are just trying to get on our feet, so we aren't reflective about where we've come from. If life was hard growing up or some things weren't right, all we did was live for that moment when we could leave and be out on our own.

Once we were on our own, we just wanted to get on with our lives and leave the past behind. So we got married, started a family, began our ministry — and ignored everything from our past. That is, until we began to see traits in ourselves that we saw expressed in others who hurt us. Or we faced a crisis and reverted to something we had never seen in ourselves before. Or we found ourselves struggling with past memories and lingering questions. We know we have issues when we get around certain people and our blood pressure begins to rise. We have to deal with our past hurts.

Preparing for New Levels of Leadership

How we handle these sediments prepares us for new levels of leadership and maturity, not to mention personal peace—if we will deal with them with:

- brutal honesty (when faced with a behavior, hurt, or crisis we have a chance to acknowledge it)
- an accurate evaluation from the Holy Spirit, God's Word, yourself, and others
- an action plan for accountability
- forgiveness

A WORD TO THE PLANTER'S SPOUSE

Blog posted by Nikki Roberts

I've worked with countless church planter wives over the past decade. There are three major concerns that always come up when church planters' wives get together.

First, what role is the spouse supposed to be playing in the church?

It's critical that both spouses are in agreement that this is what God is calling them to do. The church will dictate to you that you will "have to do it all." It all stems from the husband; he can allow the church to dictate to his wife, or he can educate the church what the wife is called to do.

There are primary and secondary ministry roles. The primary is what God has equipped you to do with your abilities and gifts. In the early days of church planting, you have to be willing to do the secondary role, which means if you have to do it, you do it but pray for leaders to take over and look for them. Sometimes when God does raise up leaders, the wives don't want to let go of the responsibility because that person doesn't share the same passion or do it as well. If someone can do it 75% as well as you can, give them the job. Let that person have the freedom to make mistakes and grow. Don't be married to a specific part of the ministry.

If you're serving in the area God has called you to serve, five things will happen. First, it will bring you joy. Second, it will bear fruit. Third, you will be affirmed. Fourth, you'll be invited to repeat it. Fifth, it will bring God glory.[1]

In deciding her roles, the husband has to let her be God-led as much as he is. Before any of it is effective, she has to share the passion of the church plant. However, you can't share the passion if you don't have personal worship time. We live in a little Christian world, so we can play the part without the passion if we aren't careful.

From personal passion comes the desire to be authentic and honest about yourself. How real is real? How much dirt do you show? Base your response on the need, not personal exhibitionism. If you're growing spiritually, you can show more and not hide.

It's also very important for her to stay on a similar learning curve with the pastor. She may not be 100% up with what he's learning, but she has to process with him, which involves communication. She needs to be able to ask questions, process — and he needs to be patient and not judge her for asking questions, realizing her personality is different from his. Most of the time he is more of a risk taker than she is, but he must gingerly lead her along.

Second, where do I go to find personal, private friendships?

This is the number one question. If you are living a godly life, it doesn't matter where your friends are. There are different categories of friends. You can be close friends to people in the church. Often, wives fear they'll ruin their husband's ministry over a conflict with someone in a church. They might need to be cautious in what they talk about, but they shouldn't walk in fear. Never share dirt on your husband with anybody. It's good to have lost friends and you'll treat them differently from friends with whom you minister.

I put a high value on friends that are believers but don't go to your church. I can talk about anything with them. When I need good, sound feedback I go to Rose Anne Taube, a lady my age.

We began teaching together at a school when I first moved to Fort Worth and Bob attended seminary. She has no outside or vested interest, so I can talk to her and know she'll be objective. Neither do I worry about her going to someone in the church.

When you're good friends with someone in the church and they decide to leave, be mature and take the higher ground. We all have to be forgiving. Roses are beautiful, but if a thorn pricks you, will you demolish all roses because of the thorns? The best gift a woman can give herself is friendships with other women.

Third, what is my family's role?

Nagging your husband to spend more time at home is not going to make him want to come home. Make it where he wants to spend more time with his family. The wife's attitude toward the time demands on the husband cannot be masked at home. The kids will pick up on her attitude and they'll suffer if she has a negative attitude about it. Jessica Cornelius once reminded me at a church planting conference: "Set the husband up for success in the family. Plan outings and put them on his calendar and you do the details."

Make a priority to have family time. When the husband has time available, make it work to spend time with the family. Our day was Saturday and we were always together. Because we did this when they were young, our kids continued to want to spend time with us as teenagers and young adults. The wife's attitude and passion are everything in this area.

A Word on Husbands

Ladies, here is what your church-planting husband needs from you:

- Join him on the learning curve. He is already on it, and it's critical for you to stay with him.
- Affirm him. Tell him that he's doing okay and that he's going to make it and that you believe in him.
- Grow spiritually in your own personal life.
- Be a sounding board and give a helpful critique.
- Be affectionate. There is no avoiding people getting upset with you in the ministry. Sometimes an embrace goes a long way.

What can a church planter do to make sure his wife is a priority and she doesn't get lost in the ministry? Take her on dates. Go to the movies, go out to eat, or go to a concert. Have fun. I ask couples who are struggling, "When was the last time you had a lot of fun together?" Most reveal that they haven't done things together in a long while. Sometimes you have to get out to catch your breath. If possible, take your wife with you to conferences and on other trips you make. I've done that with my children as well, and it gives some special time of bonding.

Affirm your wife publicly in the pulpit. There's nothing wrong with bragging about her. Affirming who she is and what she does is important. No one person is going to have more impact on your ministry than your wife.

Tell her privately of her worth and value. Tell her things that are true that you take for granted. My wife keeps me grounded—I'm a wild and crazy man. If it weren't for her, God only knows what I'd be doing. At the same time, I like to believe I've spiced up her life some!

Challenge her where she needs to grow, but don't ever do this in the middle of an argument! It is good to critique each other. I ask my wife to critique me, and I ask the same of my kids. Let her know the books that you're reading, and encourage her to read as well. Talk about what you're reading and learning together.

Above all, allow God to direct your wife and don't push. It's okay to offer occasional suggestions, but you won't have a happy marriage if you spend your life telling her "thus saith the Lord." Give ideas to your spouse, but make sure you let God direct them.

A Word to Parents

When I became a church planter, I knew I'd be gone a lot at night, especially at first. Each day I'd knock off at 4:00 p.m., go home and play hard with the kids, and then eat supper and be out the door again by 6:30. Those two hours were important—and when I was there, I was all there. Watching TV in the family room while everyone else is in their rooms isn't being there. There are many things parents should be doing for their children, but as a planter, you should be doing several unique things.

We had a weekly family time that we would not compromise. If it had to change, we always had a way of making it up. I remember one weekend we were broke and wanted to take the kids to do something. So we went out to the DFW airport and rode the tram. They were little, so to them it was fun. We played it up and told them, "Today we're going to ride the train tram around the airport!" They were so excited. At one point, they became a little too enthusiastic, and people were looking at us. I just smiled and said, "I'm sorry—we're from Arkansas!" Another time we laid on our backs outside the fence of the airport and watched the planes fly over us.

Challenge your kids to do what they do because they are followers of Jesus, not because they are the "preacher's kids." You want your kids to be great kids for God's sake, not just to help your job. This is a huge mistake preachers make. It makes their kids begin to think of character and following God as a show.

Take your children with you on trips. Once when I was with John Maxwell, I brought Jill along, though she fell asleep during the meeting! Ben went to Hanoi with me when he was ten and still a little chunky from childhood. I explained to him that people would come up to rub his belly, but I warned him that he couldn't get upset. By the time the week was over, when people came toward him, he'd just go ahead and stick his belly out for them to rub.

I had also told him he would have to eat whatever was put in front of him and smile. One day we were at a ceremony and the party official wanted to honor my son. He gave him the eyes and eggs of the fish—which is a delicacy in Vietnam. Before I could intervene, he had chomped them down. Later I asked, "How did you do it, Ben?"

"Dad," he replied, "I just thought of Jesus and what he went through—it wasn't that big of a deal." The next day it was a big deal, for he threw up all over the van!

Finally, teach your children how to act around influential people with whom you come in contact. Ben and Jill have grown up around people who are changing the world, and they just think that's the way people are supposed to live. This kind of lifestyle engenders creativity and a belief that they can do anything. Both Ben and Jill have studied international relations; it has become a part of who they are. Both aspire to do humanitarian projects—it's what they love.

Missional Families

I lead a small discipleship group that meets on Fridays at 6:00 a.m. Either they are involved in various ministries, or they are trying to figure out where to use their jobs and how to live missionally. Tension often develops in our meetings. People will say to me, "I wish I had a church like yours," or "How do you get your people doing all this stuff?" As if there is no struggle to it. There are always struggles. You just do it anyhow. You challenge people—you upset them—and you show them all they have. You put it on their plate to choose to serve or not serve.

The question is not, "Is my time supposed to be at home or outside home?" Your time is always at your home. You never stop being a husband or dad, and you never have a right to sidestep your responsibilities at home. The Bible deems the man who cares for others but not his own as "worse than an infidel" (1 Timothy 5:8 KJV).

The question is more along the lines of what the culture of your home is going to be. What is Christian culture (or, as I say, kingdom culture) in the home? What makes Christian culture different from that of a humanitarian, Buddhist, or Islamic culture? The concern is how to be a godly father and husband and model what God wants in all our lives.

I coached my son's football team for years. We took vacations, spent a couple of hours a day just playing with the kids, spent Saturdays together, and involved my daughter in dance classes and all the recitals that go with it. I wouldn't trade anything for those memories because they are memories of how we lived together as a family.

Too often we try to separate the personal aspects of our faith from the missional aspects of our faith. You can't do that. Christianity is an uncomfortable, challenging, comprehensive whole — it all fits together. It isn't enough to teach your children Bible stories. They need to see you live real-life Jesus stories and be as much a part of them as possible. Not just for now, but for what their faith is going to look like in the future.

The current model of "Christian family success" is not changing us or our culture. If anything, as a nation we are morally and ethically worse than ever. As lost as our culture was when we were growing up, our sons and daughters are inheriting a different world. We are being sold a culture of Christianity that is "just for me and mine"; such a culture will continue to doom us. When the kingdom flows in, it also flows out. It's a breathing and symbiotic relationship.

Each person must determine how he or she is called to incarnationally live out the gospel and the principles of the kingdom in the context of family, work, neighborhood, community, nation, and world. Everyone has different gifts, resources, and opportunities, but "to whom much is given, much is required."

Our culture seems to say, "To whom much is given, much less is given back!" As Christians, we should be out front modeling a different ethic and ethos, not swallowing the subtle lies about a costless and comfortable Christianity. As corny as it may sound, WWJD may be the most significant question you can ask. Or, as a friend of mine, Chris Seiple, says "WIJD?" (What Is Jesus Doing?). Please him, and you know you're doing his will. Don't compare yourself to anyone else. Celebrate how he's using you.

I'm glad families are wrestling with this issue. I'm not going to let families off the hook easily. I honestly believe the more successful a person is in life, the more difficult these questions become.

If you were to ask me which role, of all my roles in life, I love the best, it would be that of a father. How I love to go to a church and meet families and individuals who point to a grandparent or great-grandparent or great-great-grandparent who helped start that church.

My own children, Ben and Jill, have lived not just a theory of church planting, but a life of church planting—as children, adolescents, teens, and young adults. What better compliment than to have your child grow up to carry on the DNA and be part of a new church plant, so that it is as natural for a child to be a part of a new church as it was for their parents. Church multiplication builds a heritage of connection between parents and children, grandchildren and great-grandchildren that is passed down through generation after generation.

Visionaries and Voyagers

In the spring of 1998, a church planter friend of mine discovered the geographical place where God wanted him to put all these principles into practice. In May of that same year, he graduated from seminary and packed up a U-Haul, and he and his wife and six-month-old daughter prepared to start their new life. Before he left, I had one last conversation with him and affirmed what he was doing. I gave him a parting gift that day—a leather-bound journal to chronicle his journey in the following months. In it, I wrote the following on the first page:

> You are part of a long line of visionaries, risk-takers, and voyagers that pushes off from the dock and sets sail to uncharted areas. Never look back—you were made for this. Some like to ride waves with lots of foam—others, like you and me—though we like surfing, we love exploring, adventure, and discovery. Some men live only to accomplish—others live to be and experience. Paul, Augustine, Wycliffe, Luther, Carey, Warren, John Freeman and Bob Roberts—all have their stamp on you. But you are your own man. Hear and follow Christ alone. When it gets wild—walk out alone at night on the deck. Look up at the stars, feel the breeze and know we were once there too and you will make it.

The New Math

$P + S + C = S$

Missional families must set their priorities (P) and schedule (S) them. It may be necessary to confront (C) issues head-on, but it will be worth it down the road when you are successful (S).

THINGS I NEVER WANT YOU TO FORGET

Until you can stand up in a front of a group of people and say, "Imitate me," you have no business starting or leading a church.

If you go out and plant NorthWood, you've failed.

It's really not about church planting — it's about transformation.

May we have such an impact that it will merit the attention of historians. Upon research, the conclusion of the historians should be, "It wasn't because of any single one of them, but because of every single one of them."

You've been called to the kingdom, not called to preach.

Steal from every model, yet make sure you don't copy any one.

Start a church for the world, not some little spot on the map somewhere.

Finish it. Anyone can start a church; it takes much more to complete the task. What we need more of are not church starters but church finishers.

You have enough time in the day to get every single thing done that needs to be done.

You're not going to win the world for Christ 9:00 to 5:00, Monday through Thursday.

Any vision that doesn't require your entire life isn't a vision; it's just a thought.

If you make your family hate you for starting a church or winning the world, you did it wrong. If they hate you, what difference does starting a church make?

Journaling is creating a catalog of reflections.

It's all about the kingdom — kingdom in, kingdom out.

Converts may grow a church, but disciples change the world.

PART 4

APPENDIXES

THE CRITICAL PATH OF EVERY CHURCH PLANTING MOVEMENT

David Watson has identified nineteen characteristics that make up the critical path that every church planting movement experiences.

1. Passionate, extraordinary prayer
2. Authority of Scripture that leads to obedience
3. Household conversions, not just individual conversions
4. Making disciples, not converts
5. Obedience to the Word, not doctrine
6. Miracles
7. Intentional church planting
8. Local leadership—keeping foreigners out of the spotlight
9. Appropriate, abundant evangelism
10. Community of believers—forming believers into minimum practice groups that will become churches
11. Reaching out—missions
12. Reproducing—disciples/churches/groups—rapid incorporation of new believers that will reach out to all segments of society
13. Inside local leaders—worship in heart language
14. Authority of the Holy Spirit
15. Persecution—bold, fearless faith—suffering
16. Coaching/mentoring/training (on-the-job training)
17. Outside leaders who model/equip/watch/leave
18. Self-supporting—not allowing money to be an issue or drive it at all
19. Redeeming the local culture

TEN COMMANDMENTS OF CHURCH PLANTING MOVEMENTS

David Garrison created the Ten Commandments of CPMs.[1]

1. Immerse your community in prayer.
2. Saturate your community with the gospel.
3. Cling to God's Word.
4. Fight against foreign dependency, i.e., denominational aid.
5. Eliminate all nonreproducible elements.
6. Live the vision that you wish to fulfill.
7. Build reproduction into every believer and church.
8. Train all believers to evangelize, disciple, and plant churches.
9. Model, assist, watch, leave.
10. Discover what God is doing and join him.

---

1. David Garrison, *Church Planting Movements* (Bangalore: WIGtake Resources, 2003), 257.

VIRAL MOVEMENTS

What does it mean to be viral? Danielle Sacks of Viral Marketing Masters gave the following guidelines at a lecture I attended:[1]

Guidelines

1. Viral is the opposite of brute force. Chaos demands a nimble response. The more force you use, the less viral it becomes.
2. A virus catches on only if it forms a community where none existed. The infection feeds on fascination.
3. It is the experience that matters, not the quality of the image.
4. Strategically hide parts of the story and motivate people to figure it out.
5. Viral campaigns are nonlinear. They are interactive, addictive, and self-propagating.

The Viral Environment

1. Chaos demands a nimble response.
2. The conversation has already begun.
3. Seek out and join emerging communities.

---

1. Danielle Sacks, "Virology 101: The Campfire Method" (lecture, Viral Marketing Masters).

PERSONAL EVALUATION FORM

Note: This form is referred to in chapter 10.

NorthWood Church

1. On a scale of 1 to 10, rate morale churchwide. Explain your answer. *(10 = exceptional; 1 = unacceptable)*

_____

_____

_____

2. On a scale of 1 to 10, rate the spiritual health of our church. Explain your answer. *(10 = exceptional; 1 = unacceptable)*

_____

_____

_____

3. Three greatest strengths

_____

_____

_____

4. Three greatest weaknesses

_____

_____

_____

5. Three biggest obstacles

_____

_____

_____

6. Three things we really need to fix

_____

_____

_____

7. On a scale of 1 to 10, rate each ministry and comment on what we are doing well and where we need to improve. *(10 = exceptional; 1 = unacceptable)*

_____

_____

_____

WORSHIP _____
Comments: _____

_____

_____

PREACHING _____
Comments: _____

_____

_____

TEAMS _____
Comments: _____

_____

_____

CHILDREN _____
Comments: _____

_____

_____

YOUTH _____
Comments: _____

_____

_____

LEARNING CENTER _____
Comments: _____

_____

_____

SUPPORT GROUPS _____
Comments: _____

_____

_____

USHERS/GREETERS/PARKING ATTENDANTS _____
Comments: _____

_____

_____

ADMINISTRATION _____
Comments: _____
_____
_____

STEWARDSHIP _____
Comments: _____
_____
_____

OVERSEAS MISSIONS _____
Comments: _____
_____
_____

LOCAL MISSIONS _____
Comments: _____
_____
_____

CHURCH PLANTING _____
Comments: _____
_____
_____

8. What excites me most about NorthWood:
_____
_____
_____

9. What I see emerging:
_____
_____
_____

10. Three years from now, our church will...
_____
_____
_____

Staff Members

11. Bob's greatest strengths are ...
_____
_____
_____

12. Bob needs to …

_____

_____

_____

13. Mike needs to …

_____

_____

_____

14. Jordan needs to …

_____

_____

_____

15. Omar needs to …

_____

_____

_____

16. Randy needs to …

_____

_____

_____

Signature _____

Date _____

SUGGESTED READING

Church Planting

Conn, Harvey. *Planting and Growing Urban Churches.*
Keller, Timothy J., and J. Allen Thompson. *Redeemer Church Planter Manual.*
Malphurs, Aubrey. *Planting Growing Churches for the 21st Century.*
Moore, Ralph. *Starting a New Church.*
Murray, Stuart. *Church Planting.*
Search, Nelson, and Kerrick Thomas. *Launch: Starting a New Church from Scratch.*
Stetzer, Ed. *Planting Missional Churches.*

Missional

Bosch, David. *Transforming Mission.*
Cole, Neil. *Organic Church.*
Hirsch, Alan. *The Forgotten Ways.*
Stark, Rodney. *The Rise of Christianity.*

Business

Collins, Jim. *Built to Last.*
_____. *Good to Great.*
Katzenback, Jon R., and Douglas K. Smith. *The Wisdom of Teams.*

Leadership

Clinton, Robert. *The Making of a Leader.*
Maxwell, John. *Developing the Leader within You.*
_____. *Raising up Leaders around You.*

Discipleship

Roberts, Bob, Jr. *Transformation*.
Willard, Dallas. *The Divine Conspiracy*.

Global

Barnett, Thomas P. M. *The Pentagon's New Map*.
Cope, Landa. *The Old Testament Template: Relearning to Disciple Nations God's Way*.
Cunningham, Loren. *The Book That Changes the World*.
Freidman, Thomas. *The World Is Flat*.
Prahalad, C. K. *The Fortune at the Bottom of the Pyramid*.
Roberts, Bob, Jr. *Glocalization*.

Cross-Disciplinary Reading — Books to Make You Think

Dawkins, Richard. *The God Delusion*. (Read section entitled "Design").
Wilson, Edward O. *Consilience: The Unity of Knowledge*.

ENDNOTES

Chapter 1: Made in Asia — Jesus Movements

1. Christianpost.com — March 23, 2006, Christian news online.

2. Alan Hirsch has also called them "Jesus movements" in his book *The Forgotten Ways* (Grand Rapids: Brazos, 2007).

3. Rodney Stark, *The Rise of Christianity: How the Obscure, Marginal, Jesus Movement Became the Dominant Religious Force* (San Francisco: HarperSanFrancisco, 1997), 74.

4. Ibid., 79.

5. Ibid., 82.

6. Ibid., 84.

7. Ibid., 219.

8. Ibid., 150.

9. Malcolm Gladwell, *The Tipping Point: How Little Things Can Make a Big Difference* (Boston: Back Bay, 2002).

10. Jim Collins, *Good to Great: Why Some Companies Make the Leap ... and Others Don't* (New York: HarperCollins, 2001).

11. I wrote *Transformation* to deal with a different view of discipleship that leans more toward the creation of a "culture of the kingdom" where people grow through life and obedience instead of primarily through books and information transfer. Bob Roberts Jr., *Transformation* (Grand Rapids: Zondervan, 2006).

Chapter 2: Coming Soon — The First Global Church Planting Movement

1. Brother Yun and Paul Hattaway, *The Heavenly Man: The Remarkable True Story of Chinese Christian Brother Yun* (Grand Rapids: Kregel, 2003).

2. Wayne Grudem, *Systematic Theology* (Grand Rapids: Zondervan, 1993), 853.

3. Ibid., 855–57. Grudem is describing what I call the "glocal" church — the local and global expression of the church.

4. Ibid., 867. Grudem defines the purposes of the church in the way my church, NorthWood, defines T-Life (short for Transformed Life). Ministry to God in worship is what we call an interactive relationship with God. Ministry to believers is what we describe as transparent connections in an

accountable and loving community. Finally, the church has a ministry to the world — what we call glocal impact.

5. George Eldon Ladd, *Theology of the New Testament* (Grand Rapids: Eerdmans, 1994), 1111–19.

6. "The Kingdom is primarily the dynamic reign or kingly rule of God, and derivatively, the sphere in which the rule is experienced. In biblical idiom, the Kingdom is not identified with its subjects. They are the people of God's rule who enter it, live under it, and are governed by it. The church is the community of the Kingdom, but never the Kingdom itself. Jesus' disciples belong to the Kingdom as the Kingdom belongs to them; but they are not the Kingdom. The Kingdom is the rule of God; the church is a society of men." (Ibid.).

7. Ibid.

8. Alan Hirsch, blog from December 29, 2006.

9. Ibid.

10. Ibid.

11. It's sad to me that we have separated our view of the church from our view of Christ. I love what Jürgen Moltmann wrote about the church: "If, for the church of Christ, Christ is the 'subject' of the church, then in the doctrine of the church, Christology will become the dominant theme of ecclesiology. Every statement about the church will be a statement about Christ. Every statement about Christ also implies a statement about the church; yet the statement about Christ is not exhausted by the statement about the church because it also goes further, being directed towards the messianic kingdom which the church serves" (*The Church in the Power of the Spirit* [Minneapolis: Augsburg Fortress, 1993], 6.)

12. See www.globalengage.org.

13. "And we are his house, if we hold on to our courage and the hope of which we boast" (Hebrews 3:6).

14. "As though God were making his appeal through us ... on Christ's behalf: Be reconciled to God" (2 Corinthians 5:20).

15. 2 Corinthians 5:20.

16. David Garrison, *Church Planting Movements* (Bangalore: Wigtake Resources, 2003). You can't talk intelligently about church planting movements without studying David Garrison, just like you can't talk about missional church without studying David Bosch and Alan Hirsch. Bosch + Hirsch + Garrison = radical global transformation.

17. Garrison, *Church Planting Movements*, 21.

Chapter 3: Multiplication Is Local Church Driven

1. Matthew 25:14–30.

2. www.glocal.net.

3. *Transformation* deals with creating a culture of discipleship versus information transfer. See Bob Roberts Jr., *Transformation* (Grand Rapids: Zondervan, 2006).

Chapter 4: Starting Churches Is Not Enough

1. Paul McKaughn, Dellana O'Brien, and William O'Brien, *Choosing a Future of US Missions* (Monrovia, CA: MARC Publishers, 1998).

2. I wrote a book on the opportunity globalization has brought to the church; see Bob Roberts Jr., *Glocalization* (Grand Rapids: Zondervan, 2007).

3. Ibid., 21.

4. Ibid, 27.

Chapter 7: Totally Wild Spirits

1. My book *Transformation* (Grand Rapids: Zondervan, 2006) has a more detailed discussion on creating this culture of transformation in a local church.

2. Read about Level 5 Leadership in Jim Collins' *Good to Great* (New York: HarperCollins, 2001).

Chapter 8: Start with the Society, Not the Church

1. Harvey Kneisel, *New Life for Declining Churches* (out of print, contact Houston First Baptist Church, Houston, Texas).

Chapter 10: Starting a Church-Starting Center in Your Church

1. Michael Novak, *Business as a Calling* (New York: Free Press, 1996), 35–36.

2. James Hillman, *The Soul's Code: In Search of Character and Calling* (New York: Random, 1996), 3.

3. Myles Munroe, *In Pursuit of Purpose* (Shippensburg, PA: Destiny Image, 1992), taken from the front matter.

4. Ibid., 1–54.

5. James M. Kouzes and Barry C. Posner, *The Leadership Challenge*, 3rd ed. (San Francisco: Jossey-Bass, 2003), 93–97.

6. Aubrey Malphurs, *Developing a Vision for Ministry in the 21st Century* (Grand Rapids: Baker, 1999).

7. George Barna, *The Power of Vision* (Ventura, CA: Regal, 2003), 142.

8. Ibid., 45.

9. I have provided a sample of the personal evaluation form we use at North-Wood in Appendix 4.

10. Available at http://thinkexist.com/quotation/come_to_the_edge-he_said-they_said-we_are_afraid/147797.html

Chapter 11: More Than Just Numbers

1. Kennon Callahan, *Effective Church Finances* (San Francisco: Jossey-Bass, 1997); idem, *Giving and Stewardship in an Effective Church* (San Francisco: Jossey-Bass, 1997 [reprint ed.]).

2. Callahan, *Giving and Stewardship*, 65–80.

3. Ibid., 65–80.

Chapter 12: Living as a Missional Family

1. See Elisabeth George, *Life Management for Busy Women* (Eugene, OR: Harvest House, 2002), 214–15.

INDEX